The Ultimate Asian Cookbook

Emma Callery

CHARTWELL
BOOKS, INC.

A QUANTUM BOOK

This edition published in 2011 by

CHARTWELL BOOKS, INC.

A division of BOOK SALES, INC.

276 Fifth Avenue, Suite 206

New York, New York 10001

USA

ISBN-13: 978-0-7858-2847-1

QUMTUAC

This book is produced by

Quantum Publishing

6 Blundell Street

London N7 9BH

Digitized by Quadrum Solutions, Mumbai, Indian

www.quadrumltd.com

Cover design by Dave Jones, www.euro-designs.info

Consultant Editors: Emma Callery and Caroline Smith

Managing Editor: Julie Brooke

Project Editor: Samantha Warrington

Assistant Editor: Jo Morley

Production Manager: Rohana Yusof

Publisher: Sarah Bloxham

Printed in Singapore by

Star Standard Industries Pte Ltd

The material in this publication previously appeared in *Complete Chinese Cookbook*,
Step-by-Step Japanese Cooking, *Hot & Spicy Cookbook*, *The Soy for Health Cookbook*, *Chinese Regional
Cooking*, *Classic Chinese and Oriental Cooking*, *Chinese Cookery Masterclass*, *Chinese Vegetarian Cooking*

Contents

INTRODUCTION

The Regional Cooking Styles of China

Looking at a map of China, it is not difficult to understand why there should be such a large variety of different cooking styles throughout the country. The Chinese attach great importance to the use of fresh meat and tender young vegetables, so, as it was difficult to transport food and keep it fresh, each region was forced to make the best use of its own products. Every district has its own speciality, yet all these different forms and styles of cooking can be grouped into "schools": Beijing, Shanghai, Sichuan and Guangzhou (Canton).

BEIJING (Northern School)
Besides the local cooking of Hebei (the province Beijing is situated in), Beijing cuisine embraces the cooking styles of Shandong, Henan and Shanxi, as well as the Chinese Muslim cooking of Inner Mongolia and Xinjiang.
Specialities: *Beijing duck, Mongolian hotpot.*

SHANGHAI (Eastern School)
Also known as the Huaiyang School of the Yangtze River delta, with Shanghai as its culinary center. This region covers the fertile lands of Anhui, Jiangsu and Fujian. (Fujian forms a school of its own, but is sometimes linked with the Southern School).

The provinces of Hubei and Jiangxi are sometimes grouped here as they both belong to China's "Lands of Fish and Rice."
Specialities: *White-cut pork, lions' heads, squirrel fish.*

SICHUAN (Western School)
The "red basin" of Sichuan is one of the richest lands of China. Owing to its geographical position, it was practically inaccessible from the rest of China until recently, therefore it developed a very distinct style of cooking. Its richly flavored and piquant food has influenced the neighboring provinces of Hunan and Guizhou.

Sichuan food has only comparatively recently been introduced to the outside world, but now has a strong following in many Western countries.
Specialities: *tea-smoked duck, chili dishes, eggplant in "fish sauce."*

CANTON (Southern School)
The Pearl River delta, with Canton as the capital of Guangdong, is undoubtedly the home of the most famous of all Chinese cooking styles, as it also embraces Hong Kong. Unfortunately its reputation has been damaged by a great number of so-called "chop suey" houses outside China. Authentic Cantonese food has no rival and has a greater variety of dishes than any other school. As Canton was the first Chinese port opened for trade, foreign influences are particularly strong in its cooking.
Specialities: *cha shao, roast suckling pig; also famous for its dim sum (snacks).*

Above: A typical Chinese market scene

The Elements of Taste

Above: The different flavors and textures so important in Chinese cooking, including Chinese chives.

"Everyone eats and drinks," said Confucius, "but few can appreciate taste." Since taste is a very personal thing (just as "beauty is in the eye of the beholder"), one's palate has to be developed both physically and intellectually. Few people in the West, however, are aware that, for centuries, Chinese scholars discussed, analyzed and wrote down their thoughts on food and drink, and that some of them developed an extensive knowledge of the nature of food and the physiology of taste based on Taoist and Confucianist teachings.

No one would disagree that the essence of the art of cooking lies in the taste of food. The Chinese believe the most important elements that help us to appreciate the taste are color, aroma, flavor and texture. All these elements have to be well balanced to form a harmonious whole, and this is the central principle of culinary art.

Any wine connoisseur will immediately recognize the parallel with wine tasting: first you examine the color, then smell the bouquet, next you taste the flavor and, finally, you judge its body and aftertaste. This may sound very elementary to the expert, but how many uneducated palates can truly appreciate the subtleties of all these elements when they are combined in a single dish?

Above left: Tofu

Above right: Succulent Beijing ducks prepared for deepfrying.

Left: Some of the many varieties of Chinese cabbage.

Above: Eggplants

COLOR

Each ingredient has its own color. Some change color when cooked, others only show their true color when contrasted with different colored ingredients.

AROMA

Aroma and flavor are very closely related to each other, and they both form an essential element in the taste experience. The agents a Chinese cook most often uses to bring out the true aroma of a certain ingredient are: scallions, root ginger, garlic and wine—the four essential flavors.

FLAVOR

Each region has its own classification of flavors, but out of scores of subtle taste experiences, the Chinese have isolated five primary flavors: sweet, sour, salty, bitter and piquant. They have also learned how to combine some of these flavors to create an entirely new flavor—sweet and sour, for instance, make an interesting pair, but not sweet and piquant or sour and bitter.

TEXTURE

This is another vital element in Chinese cooking. A dish should have one texture or several textures: tenderness, crispness, crunchiness, smoothness or softness. The selection of different textures in a single dish is as important as the blending of different flavors and the contrast of complementary colors.

HARMONY

Very few Chinese dishes consist of only a single ingredient; as it offers no contrast it therefore lacks harmony. This is the basic Taoist philosophy of yin and yang. So, with few exceptions, all Chinese dishes consist of a main ingredient (be it pork, beef, chicken or fish) with one or several supplementary ingredients (usually vegetables) to give the dish the desired harmonious balance of color, aroma, flavor and texture.

For instance, if the main ingredient is pork, which is pale pink in color and tender in texture, one would use either celery (pale green and crunchy) or green peppers (dark green and crisp) as the supplementary ingredient; or one might choose mushrooms (Chinese mushrooms are much darker in color with a soft texture) or bamboo shoots (pale yellow and crunchy), or a combination of both.

This principle of harmonious contrast is carried all the way through a meal. No Chinese would serve just a single dish on his table, however humble his circumstances might be. The order in which different dishes are served, either singly or in pairs (often in fours), is strictly governed by the same principles: avoid monotony and do not serve similar types of food one after another or together, but use contrasts to create a perfect harmony.

VEGETARIAN COOKING

Vegetarian cooking has a long history in China. Traditionally the Chinese have always been highly aware of, indeed one would almost say obsessed by, the link between food and health, whether physical or spiritual. Consequently many Chinese follow a vegetarian diet on health rather than economic grounds, although many are Buddhists who abhor the killing of any living creature and would certainly never dream of eating meat or fish in any form.

The close associations between Buddhists and the nonbeliever vegetarians are deep-rooted. One interesting point to note here is that despite their continual introduction, milk and dairy products are, to date, not prominent in Chinese cuisine. Therefore, unlike their counterparts in the West, Chinese vegetarians will not use butter, cheese or milk in their cooking, and a true Buddhist will eat neither eggs nor fish.

The art of cooking vegetables has been perfected by the Chinese—the vegetables are almost always done lightly and simply. Obviously, different types of vegetables should be treated differently: a few require longer cooking time; others need to be cooked with more than one ingredient to achieve the correct "cross-blending" of flavors.

Thai Cooking

Just as with Chinese food, the aim of the Thai cook is to achieve harmony in a meal; the dishes served should be a perfect balance of flavors, colors and textures. The combination of different ingredients should bring out the natural flavor of the foods used.

Above: A vendor sells fresh produce at a Bangkok floating market.

THAI FLAVORS

Thai food is often characterized as spicy, but there is a lot more to the cuisine than that. Although chilies are used in many dishes, there are plenty of other ingredients that bring great variety to Thai meals. Lemongrass is one of the significant herbs used, adding a zesty flavor to dishes. Kaffir lime leaves also have a tangy, citrusy taste. These dark green, shiny leaves, with their unusual figure-of-eight shape, are torn or cut into small shreds.

Galangal is used in Thai food much in the same way as ginger is in other Oriental cuisines. If you can't get hold of fresh galangal, substitute fresh ginger. No description of Thai food would be complete without mention of *nam pla*, the salty fish sauce used to flavor many dishes. Thai food also uses many ingredients common to other Asian cooking styles; coconut milk, soy sauce, fresh cilantro, spring onions and garlic, to name but a few.

FRESH INGREDIENTS

Thailand is a fertile country with a tropical climate, and so a varied range of produce is available all year round—salads of raw fruit and vegetables are often served. It has a long coastline and the interior of the country is blessed with freshwater lakes and rivers, and so fish and seafood are the key source of animal protein in Thai cooking, with poultry and other meats being secondary.

As in other Asian cultures, rice and noodles are the key staples of Thai cooking. Breakfast might be a bowl of rice soup, while lunch is often noodles, served in a soup or stir-fried with vegetables. The evening meal is usually the main meal of the day and it will be centred around a large bowl of rice. When cooking a Thai meal yourself, look for fragrant Thai rice.

MEALS IN THAILAND

A Thai evening meal consists of several dishes—at least four—served all at once. One of these dishes will be a soup of some kind, made from seafood, vegetables or chicken; one will be a main dish, featuring fish, vegetables, poultry or meat; one will be salad of raw vegetables or fruit (or a combination of both), dressed with a spicy sauce; and the last will be a bowl of rice. The soup is served in individual bowls but all the other dishes are placed in the centre of the table so that individual diners can help themselves.

Puddings are not really a feature of Thai meals, although fresh fruit may be served to finish. Cakes and sweets are made in Thai cooking, but these are eaten as snacks rather than as part of a meal. Generally speaking, Thai food is eaten with spoons and forks—knives are unnecessary since ingredients are chopped into small pieces during the preparation of dishes. Chopsticks are used, but these are reserved for the eating of noodles.

In Thailand, iced tea or water is usually served with a meal; alcohol, in the form of a glass of spirits, is served as an aperitif. If you want to drink wine with a Thai meal, then look for one with a slight sweetness, such as a Gewürztraminer or Riesling. Or serve a sparkling white—a demi-sec cava or champagne rather than a brut. A Thai beer would also be ideal.

Japanese Cooking

Japanese food is characterized by the great care taken in its preparation and presentation. Although meals are made up of essentially simple ingredients, each dish is a work of art in itself. Colors, textures and tastes are combined to create a unique cuisine.

FISH AND TOFU

As an island nation, for the Japanese fish and seafood are a vital part of their diet and remain the key source of protein. Cooking methods are extremely varied for every kind of fish and sea creature.

Tofu, also known as bean curd, is the next most important source of protein. This is made by processing soy beans until they form a thick, set curd with a delicate flavor and a texture similar to a stiff blancmange. Tofu has been referred to in the West as Japanese cheese, but it is much lower in fat, is cholesterol free, and is higher in protein and vitamins than milk cheeses.

RICE AND NOODLES

As with other Asian cuisines, rice is the staple of Japanese food and it features in virtually every meal. The rice of choice in Japan is a short-grain rice that is stickier and more glutinous than long-grain rice.

Noodles are eaten almost as frequently as rice and are served with a sauce or in a soup. They are made from either wheat flour (udon) or buckwheat (soba). In a typical Japanese meal, the portions of the other dishes are small in size, but diners fill up with large bowls of rice or noodles.

JAPANESE FLAVORS

Japanese food features a range of unique ingredients as well as some which are similar to, or the same as, other Asian cooking styles. Typically Japanese is miso, a flavoring made from fermented soy, wheat or barley that is added to soups and stocks.

The main stock is dashi, made from kombu seaweed. Other seaweeds play an important role too; most well-known is nori, used in thin sheets to wrap around other ingredients to make sushi.

Japanese soy sauce is slightly sweeter than the Chinese variety, with a more sherry-like flavor. Another typically Japanese condiment is mirin, a type of fortified rice wine with a sweet flavor. Hot and spicy flavors are obtained from gari, a type of pickled ginger, and wasabi, a pungent, green paste that is sometimes known as Japanese horseradish.

A key feature of these ingredients is umami, a Japanese word meaning "savory flavor." This word is now used in the west as the name of the fifth basic taste (along with salty, sour, bitter and sweet) and to describe those foods which are particularly savory in flavor and which leave a sense of fullness in the mouth, such as tomatoes and Parmesan cheese.

COOKING AND EATING

Japanese dishes are classified by the cooking techniques used. Steamed foods are mushimono, grilled foods are yakimono and deep-fried dishes are agemono. Dishes where ingredients are poached—and where the poaching liquid is drunk—are known as nimon. Sushi—probably the most famous of Japan's dishes—are made from cakes of rice topped with fish or other foods. Raw fish served with wasabi is sashimi.

Formal meals in Japan are characterized by the care taken in presenting food. The bowls and plates in which the food is served and eaten are chosen to either contrast with or complement the various treats on offer. The idea is to create harmony at the table. Food is eaten with chopsticks—the ends of Japanese chopsticks taper to more of a point than Chinese ones—and chopsticks are laid on the table with matching rests; it is bad manners in Japan to leave your chopsticks on the edge of your plate or on the table.

Above: Typical Japanese tableware and chopsticks.

Special Ingredients

BAMBOO SHOOTS
In the West, bamboo shoots are available in cans, which is a pity since, when tinned, they lose much of their crisp texture and flavor. Once the can is opened, the shoots may be kept in a covered jar of water in the fridge for several days. Braised bamboo shoots in cans should be eaten cold without any further cooking.

DASHI
Dashi is a type of stock made from seaweed and, usually, preserved tuna. It may also be made with dried sardines or shiitake. Instant dashi—in powder or liquid form—is widely available and is the most commonly used form in Japan.

TOFU
Made from soaked yellow soy beans ground with water. A coagulant is added after some of the water is strained through muslin, causing the ground beans to curdle and become firm tofu. Usually sold in squares about 6¼ x 6¼ cm (2½ x 2½ in), 1½ cm (¼ in) thick. It will keep a few days if submerged in water in a container and placed in the coldest part of the fridge. Dried tofu skin is usually sold either in thick sticks or thin sheets. It

should be soaked in cold water overnight or in warm water for at least an hour before use.

BEANSPROUTS
Two kinds are available: yellow soy beansprouts, only to be found in Chinese grocers, and green mung beansprouts, which can be bought from almost every large supermarket. (Never use tinned beansprouts; they do not have the crunchy texture that is the main characteristic of beansprouts). They can be kept in the fridge for two or three days if bought fresh. See also mung beans.

BLACK BEAN SAUCE
Sometimes called crushed bean sauce, this thick sauce is made from black beans, flour and salt. It is sold in cans and, once opened, must be transferred into a screw-top jar and then it will keep in a fridge for months. It has a distinctive salty taste.

CELLOPHANE OR TRANSPARENT GLASS NOODLES
Made from mung beans. They are sold in dried form, the noodles tied into bundles weighing from 60–450 g (2–16 oz). Soak in warm water for five minutes before use.

CHILI PASTE
Also called chili purée. Made of chili, soy bean, salt, sugar and flour. It is sold in jars and will keep almost indefinitely.

CHILI SAUCE
Hot, red sauce made from chilies, vinegar, plums, salt and sesame.

CHINESE CABBAGE

There are innumerable varieties of cabbage grown in China, of which only two or three types are available in the West. The one most commonly seen is known as celery cabbage or Chinese leaves: it has a pale green color and tightly wrapped elongated head; two-thirds of the vegetable is stem that has a crunchy texture. Another variety has a shorter and fatter head with curlier pale yellow leaves. Then there is the dark green-leaved variety, also with white stems, and the bright green-leaved variety with pale green stems, sometimes with a sprig of yellow flower in the center, which is very much prized by the Chinese. These last two varieties are sold only in Chinese shops.

CHINESE DRIED MUSHROOMS

There are two main types of Chinese mushrooms:

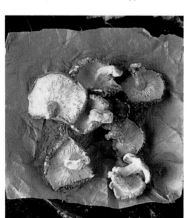

those that grow on trees, known as fragrant or winter mushrooms, and those cultivated on a bed of straw, known as straw mushrooms. Fragrant or winter mushrooms are sold dried; they are used in many dishes as a complementary vegetable for their flavor and aroma. Soak in warm water for 20–30 minutes, squeeze dry and discard the hard stalks before use. Straw mushrooms are available in cans, but are completely different in texture and flavor. The Western varieties of common or field mushrooms can be used as substitutes, but they do not impart as much flavor.

DRIED SHRIMP

These are small to very small, and are sold cleaned, shelled and whole. They add a salty, savory seasoning to dishes.

FIVE-SPICE POWDER

A mixture of aniseed, fennel, cloves, cinnamon and pepper. It is very strongly piquant, so use a very small amount at a time. It will keep for years if stored in a tightly covered container.

FISH SAUCE

This is made from fish that have been allowed to ferment; the type of fish used depends on the country or region of origin. Fish sauce has a pungent, salty flavor is used as a condiment throughout Asia.

GALANGAL

Related to root ginger and with a similar flavor, galangal is used in Thai cooking. It is prepared in much the same way as ginger.

FRESH GINGER ROOT

Sold by weight. Should be peeled and sliced or finely chopped before use. Will keep for weeks in a dry, cool place. Dried and powdered ginger is not a satisfactory substitute for fresh ginger.

GLUTEN

A high-gluten flour and water dough is soaked and kneaded in water to wash out the starch; the remaining gluten is porous like a sponge. It is cut into pieces to be used like dumplings to carry flavor and provide bulk in sauces.

GREEN CHILI

Will keep fresh for a week or two in the vegetable compartment of the fridge in a plastic bag.

GREEN SEAWEED

This moss-like seaweed is dark green in color. It is sold dried, in wads or in matted crisps. When deep-fried in oil, it is crisp and has a toasted fragrance. Dried green cabbage leaves can be used as a substitute.

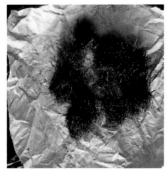

HOISIN SAUCE

Also known as barbecue sauce. Made from soy beans, sugar, flour, vinegar, salt, garlic, chili and sesame.

KAFFIR LIME LEAVES

The leaves of the kaffir lime have a fresh citrusy flavor. They can be used fresh or dried and freeze well.

KAOLIANG SPIRIT

A spirit made from sorghum and millet. Brandy or vodka can be substituted.

LEMONGRASS

Another essential in Thai cooking, lemongrass has a clean, slightly lemony flavor. Discard the ends and the dark green parts and then chop finely to use.

MIRIN

A sweet rice wine, similar to sake but with a lower alcohol content. It's used in Japanese cooking.

MISO

A flavoring used in Japanese cooking and made from fermented soy, rice or barley. You will find white miso, red miso and mixed miso available.

MONOSODIUM GLUTAMATE (MSG)

A chemical compound often used to heighten flavor but which can wipe out subtle taste distinctions.

MUNG BEANS

A small green bean used for making mung bean noodles (see Cellophane Noodles) or for sprouting. They are available from Chinese groceries and many large supermarkets.

OYSTER SAUCE

A thick sauce made from oysters and soy sauce. Sold in bottles, it will keep in the fridge indefinitely.

RED BEAN PASTE

A thick sauce made from fermented bean curd and salt. Sold in tins or jars, it will keep indefinitely.

Above: 1 Shaoxing wine **2** Groundnut oil **3** Vinegar **4** Monosodium glutamate **5** Sesame oil **6** Oyster sauce

RICE CAKES (mochi)

Mochi, or rice cakes, are made from glutinous rice which is pounded into a thick paste and then formed into the cake shapes. A traditional Japanese food, they do feature in other Asian cuisines.

RICE WINE

Also known as Shaoxing wine, made from glutinous rice. Sake or pale (medium or dry) sherry can be substituted.

SALTED BLACK BEANS

Whole bean sauce, very salty.

SESAME OIL

Sold in bottles. Widely used in China as a garnish rather than for cooking. The refined yellow sesame oil sold in Middle Eastern stores has less flavor and therefore is not a very satisfactory substitute.

SESAME PASTE

In Oriental cooking, this paste is made from toasted sesame seeds which gives it a different flavor to the Mediterranean version, tahini. Thicker than tahini, it's more like peanut butter in texture.

SHRIMP PASTE

This is made by pulverising fermented shrimps. The resulting paste is dried and cut into blocks. It adds a fishy, salty flavor to food and is used in several different Asian cuisines.

SOY SAUCE

Sold in bottles or cans, this liquid ranges from light to dark brown in color. The darker colored sauces are strongest and more often used in cooking, whereas the lighter ones are used at the table.

SICHUAN PEPPERCORNS

These reddish-brown peppercorns, are much stronger than either the black or white peppercorns of the West. Sold in plastic bags, they will keep indefinitely in a tightly sealed container.

DRIED GOLDEN NEEDLES (dried Tiger Lily buds)

The buds of a special type of lily. Sold in dried form, they should be soaked in warm water for 10–20 minutes and the hard stems removed. They are often used in combination with wood ears.

WATER CHESTNUTS

Water chestnuts do not belong to the chestnut family, they are the roots of a vegetable. They are available fresh or in tins. They keep for about a month in a fridge, in a covered jar.

WHITE NUTS

Also known as ginkgo nuts, they are the pits or nuts of the fruits from the ginkgo tree. Available tinned, they are very popular with Chinese vegetarians.

Above: 1 Hoisin sauce **2** Salted black beans **3** Light soy sauce **4** Dark soy sauce **5** Red bean-curd sauce **6** Crushed yellow bean sauce **7** Yellow bean sauce

WOOD EARS

Also known as cloud ears or tree fungus. Sold dried, they should be soaked in warm water for 20 minutes; discard any hard stems and rinse in fresh water before use.

YELLOW BEAN SAUCE

This thick sauce is made from crushed yellow beans, flour and salt. It is sold in cans or jars; once opened, it should be transferred into a screw-top jar. It will keep in the fridge for months.

WAKAME SEAWEED

This edible seaweed is popular in Japanese cooking, although it is also used in some regions of China. It can be found in both fresh or dried forms and is often added to soups.

POULTRY

Chickens, ducks and geese have been reared as food in Asia for centuries, millennia even; there is evidence that domesticated chickens were being eaten in China as long as five thousand years ago. Chicken can be stirfried, steamed, boiled or roasted, though duck and goose are more often roasted. Some of the most delicious dishes in Asian cooking feature poultry—Chicken Kung-Po Style and Beijing Duck with Pancakes, to name but two.

Stirfried Chicken with Garlic and Cucumber

Serves 5–6

6 chicken breasts	2 scallions
1 medium cucumber	3 tbsp vegetable oil
1 tsp salt	2 slices fresh ginger
pepper to taste	½ tsp salt
4 tsp cornstarch	1½ tbsp rice wine
½ egg white	or dry sherry
2 cloves garlic	1 tbsp light
1 tbsp lard	soy sauce
2 tbsp stock	½ tsp sesame oil

1 Cut the chicken into 1¼ cm (½ in) cubes. Cut the cucumber into similar-sized cubes. Sprinkle and rub the chicken evenly with 1 tsp of salt, pepper and half the cornstarch, then wet with egg white. Crush the garlic. Chop the lard. Blend the remaining cornstarch with the stock. Cut the scallions into 1.25 cm (1½ in) sections.

2 Heat the vegetable oil in a wok or frying pan. When hot, stir in ginger slices for 15 seconds to flavor the oil. Remove and discard the ginger. Add the chicken cubes to the pan and stirfry over a medium to high heat for 45 seconds. Remove and drain.

3 Add the lard and garlic to the pan and stir over medium heat for 15 seconds. Add the cucumber cubes and sprinkle with the 1 tsp of salt and pepper. Stirfry for 1 minute. Add the rice wine or sherry, soy sauce and scallions.

4 Blend the sesame oil and remaining flour together. Return the chicken to the saucepan and stirfry for 1 minute. Add the blended cornstarch and sesame oil and stirfry for 10 seconds. Serve.

Golden Chicken with Shrimp Paste

Serves 6–8

1–1½ g (3–38 oz) fresh chicken
2–3 tbsp shrimp paste (fresh shrimps, finely ground)
700 ml (1½ pt) peanut oil

Marinade

3 tbsp cornstarch
1 tbsp rice wine or dry sherry
2 tsp ginger juice (squeezed from ginger puréed in a blender)
1 tsp sugar
few drops sesame oil

1 Chop the chicken into large, bite-sized pieces and pat them dry.

2 Mix the shrimp paste with the marinade ingredients, and marinate the chicken with the mixture for 20 minutes.

3 Heat the peanut oil in a saucepan and fry the chicken pieces over medium heat for 2 minutes to cook them through. Remove the chicken and set the pieces aside while you reheat the oil, fry the chicken, this time on the high heat for 1½ minutes until golden, serve.

Quickly Braised Chicken with Green Chilies, Green Peppers and Black Beans

Serves 4–6

900 g (2 lb) chicken
cornstarch
3 green peppers
2 fresh green chilies
1 small piece dried
   orange peel
2 cups peanut oil
2 tbsp fermented,
   salted soy beans
1 tsp chopped garlic
90 g (3 oz) shallots,
   chopped
2 tsp rice wine

Seasonings

3 tsp stock
1 tsp salt
1 tsp monosodium
   glutamate
   (optional)
1 tsp sugar
2 tsp dark soy sauce
1 tbsp cornstarch
   blended with
   3 tbsp water

1 Chop the chicken through the bones into large, bite-sized pieces and dust with cornstarch.
2 Cut the peppers and chilies into slices, and soak the dried orange peel before shredding it.
3 Heat the saucepan until it is very hot. Pour in the peanut oil and fry the chicken until it starts to turn brown.
4 Heat a clay pot or casserole dish until it is very hot. Pour 2 tbsp peanut oil into it and add the chilies, peppers, fermented beans, chopped garlic and shallots to sauté, stirring them together until fragrant.
5 Add the chicken pieces and sprinkle with rice wine. Sauté for 30 seconds more.
6 Blend the seasonings and add to the pot. Stir and cover the container to cook for 30 seconds over high heat. Keep the container covered until ready to serve.

Cantonese Fried Chicken

Serves 4–6
1.3 kg (3 lb) young chicken
2 tbsp soy sauce
1 tbsp rice wine or sherry
oil for deep frying

Sauce
2 scallions, finely chopped
2 slices fresh ginger, peeled and finely chopped
1 tbsp sugar
1 tbsp vinegar

1   Clean the chicken well; parboil in a large pot of boiling water for 2–3 minutes; remove and drain.
2   Marinate in soy sauce and rice wine or sherry for 20–30 minutes.
3   Heat up the oil in a deep fryer; brown the chicken all over, basting constantly for 20–30 minutes. Leave it to cool before chopping into small pieces. Arrange neatly on a serving dish.
4   Add the remains of the marinade to the sauce mixture, bring to a boil and simmer for 5 minutes; either pour it over the chicken as a suace, or serve it as a dip.

Multi-flavored Chicken

Serves 8–10
1.75–2.25 kg (4–5 lb)
   fresh chicken

Sauce
2 tbsp sesame oil
1 tsp malt vinegar
1 tsp sugar
1 tbsp chili sauce
1 tbsp chopped
   garlic
1 tsp ground
   peppercorns
3 tbsp grated
   spring onions
½ tsp salt
8 tbsp stock

1   Clean the chicken thoroughly. Put 6 cups water into a saucepan and bring to a boil. Add the chicken and simmer for 10 minutes over low heat. Remove the chicken and rinse for 2 minutes. Return the chicken to the water and boil for 5 more minutes. Rinse with cold water again.
2   Remove the bones from the chicken and handshred the meat, arranging the shredded chicken on a plate.
3   Blend together the ingredients for the sauce. Pour it over the chicken on the dish and serve.

Shanghai Quick-braised Chicken on the Bone

Serves 6–8

1.5–2 kg (3–4 lb) chicken	2 tbsp sugar
1 tbsp cornstarch	1 tbsp hoisin sauce
4 tbsp vegetable oil	1 tbsp oyster sauce
5 slices fresh ginger	4 tbsp rice wine or dry sherry
3 tbsp light soy sauce	500 ml (1 pt) good stock
3 tbsp dark soy sauce	scallions to garnish

1 Chop the chicken through the bone into about 30 bite-sized pieces. Bring a large saucepan of water to a boil, add the chicken and simmer for about 5 minutes. Remove and drain thoroughly. Blend the cornstarch with 3 tbsp of water.

2 Heat the oil in a wok or saucepan. When hot, stir in the ginger for about 1½ minutes. Add the chicken pieces and stirfry for about 3 minutes. Put in the, soy sauces, sugar, hoisin sauce, oyster sauce, wine or sherry and stock. Bring to a boil and continue to stir over the highest heat until the sauce begins to thicken and reduce. Add the blended flour and stir until the sauce is thick and coats the chicken pieces. Garnish with the scallions, grated or decoratively cut.

Melon Chicken

Serves 6–8

3 large dried Chinese mushrooms	1.25–1.5 kg (2½–3 lb) chicken
2 tbsp dried shrimps	2 tbsp vegetable oil
1 large melon, approximately 20.5 cm (8 in) in diameter	2 slices fresh ginger
	90 g (3 oz) button mushrooms
	1 tsp salt
90 g (3 oz) ham	pepper to taste
120 ml (4 fl oz) tinned bamboo shoots, drained	stock cube crumbled into 300 ml (10 fl oz) water
	2 tbsp dry sherry

1 Soak the dried mushrooms and dried shrimp separately in hot water to cover for 25 minutes. Slice the top of the melon off and reserve for a lid. Scrape out most of the flesh and reserve about a quarter for cooking with the chicken. Drain and discard the tough mushroom stalks. Cut the mushroom caps into quarters. Cut the ham and bamboo shoots into cubes.

2 Place the chicken in a steamer and steam for about 1 hour. Leave to cool. When cool enough to handle, remove the meat from the bones and cut into cubes. Heat the oil in a wok or large frying pan. When hot, stirfry the ginger, dried shrimp and dried mushrooms over high heat for about 2 minutes. Add the ham, half of the chicken, the bamboo shoots, reserved melon, fresh mushrooms, salt and pepper. Stirfry for 3 minutes more. Pack all the stirfried ingredients into the melon. Add any excess to the remaining chicken. Mix the crumbled stock cube with the stock and sherry and pour into the melon to the brim. Replace melon lid and fasten with a few wooden toothpicks. Place on a heatproof plate and steam for 30 minutes.

3 Bring the whole melon to the table to serve. This is a pretty dish and the different savory flavors in the chicken-ham-mushroom stuffing and the sweetness of the melon give it a unique appeal.

White-cut Chicken

Serves 6–8
1.5 kg (3 lb) chicken
2 slices fresh ginger
2 scallions

Sauce
1 clove garlic, crushed
1 slice fresh ginger, peeled
1 scallion
1 tsp salt
1 tsp sugar
2 tbsp soy sauce
½ tbsp sesame oil

1 Clean the chicken and place it in a large pot with enough water to cover. Add the fresh ginger and scallions; cover the pot with a tight-fitting lid and bring it to a boil. Simmer for 5 minutes, then turn off the heat and let the chicken cook gently in the hot water for 3–4 hours. Do not lift the lid while you wait for it to cool.

2 To serve, remove the chicken and drain. Chop it into 20–24 pieces, then reassemble on a long dish. Leave to cool to room temperature.

3 Finely chop the garlic, fresh ginger and scallion; mix with salt, sugar, soy sauce, sesame oil and a little stock. Either pour it all over the chicken or use as a dip.

Chili Chicken

Serves 4–6
230 g (8 oz) chicken breast meat, boned
1 egg white
½ tsp salt
½ tbsp cornstarch
1 slice fresh ginger, peeled
1 clove garlic
2 scallions, white parts only
1 small green pepper
1 small red pepper
1 tbsp rice wine or sherry
1 tbsp soy sauce
3 tbsp stock
oil for deep frying
1 tbsp chili paste
½ tsp sesame seed oil

1 Dice the chicken into 1.25 cm (½ in) cubes, mix with the egg white, salt and ½ tbsp cornstarch.

2 Cut the fresh ginger and garlic into thin slices; cut the scallions diagonally into short lengths. Cut the green and red peppers into small squares roughly the same size as the chicken cubes.

3 Mix together the rice wine or sherry, soy sauce, stock and the remaining cornstarch in a bowl.

4 Heat up the oil and deep fry the chicken cubes until pale golden; scoop out and drain.

5 Pour off the excess oil, leaving about 1 tbsp in the wok; toss in the fresh ginger, garlic, scallions, green and red peppers, the chicken and chili paste. Stir a few times.

6 Now add the sauce mixture to the wok; blend well; add the sesame oil just before serving.

Purse Chicken Dumplings

Makes about 20 "purses"
260 g (9 oz) broccoli
1 tbsp salt
2 medium black mushrooms, dried
40 g (1½ oz) bamboo shoots
60 g (2 oz) water chestnuts
1 tbsp salt
5 tbsp peanut oil
3 scallions
140 g (5 oz) chicken breast
2 tsp egg white
½ tbsp cornstarch
1 tbsp fresh cilantro, stem and leaf, chopped
strands of scallion
2 tbsp crab roe

Wrappers
3 egg whites
2 tsp cornstarch
3 tbsp chicken stock

Sauce
180 ml (6 fl oz) chicken stock
1 tsp sesame oil
2 tsp Chinese yellow wine
1 tsp salt

1   Cut the broccoli into shavings, wash in salted water and set aside.
2   Soak the black mushrooms in hot water for 30 minutes. Remove and discard the stems, finely chop the caps and set aside.
3   Finely chop the bamboo shoots and water chestnuts and set aside. Bring 240 ml (8 fl oz) water to a boil, add 1 tbsp salt and 1 tbsp oil and cook the broccoli spears for 5 minutes. Blanch the scallions for 30 seconds. Remove and set aside.
4   Dice the chicken finely and mix it with 2 tsp egg white and ½ tsp cornstarch. Set aside.
5   Heat 2 tbsp oil in saucepan. Add the black mushrooms, water chestnuts, bamboo shoots, cilantro and the chicken mixture. Stir and cook for 1½ minutes over low heat. Remove, drain and set aside.
6   Mix together the wrapper ingredients. Heat a frying pan and grease the bottom with oil. Spoon 1 tbsp of the mixture into the center of the pan and make a thin pancake over low heat. Repeat this process until all the mixture is used up.
7   Take one wrapper and spoon 1 tbsp of the chicken and vegetable filling into the center, gather up the edges and tie the top of the bundle with a strand of scallion (use the green part only). Put ⅓ tsp crab roe on top in the center of the bundle.
8   Arrange the purses in the center of a plate, sprinkle with broccoli and steam over medium heat for 5 minutes.
9   Heat 2 tbsp oil in a saucepan and add the sauce ingredients. Bring the sauce to a boil, stir and pour it over the chicken dumplings before serving.

Stirfried Chicken and Celery on Rice

Serves 4–6

2–3 medium
   dried Chinese
   mushrooms
1 chicken breast
1 celery stick
80 ml (2⅔ fl oz)
   tinned bamboo
   shoots, drained
2 slices fresh ginger
2 scallions

3 tbsp vegetable oil
salt and pepper
   to taste
2 tbsp good stock
2 tbsp rice wine or
   dry sherry
1 tbsp light soy sauce
240 ml (8 fl oz)
   boiled rice

1. Soak the dried mushrooms in hot water to cover for 25 minutes. Drain and discard the tough stalks. Cut the mushroom caps into small cubes. Dice the chicken into small cubes. Dice the celery and bamboo shoots into similar-sized cubes. Finely chop the ginger. Chop the scallions.

2. Heat the oil in a wok or frying pan. When hot, stirfry the ginger, scallions, mushrooms, celery and bamboo shoots over high heat for 1 minute. Add the chicken and stirfry for 1 minute. Sprinkle with salt and pepper to taste. Add the stock, rice wine or sherry and soy sauce, toss and turn for one more minute.

3. Serve on boiled rice. If desired, wrap spoonfuls of chicken and rice in lettuce leaves to eat with the fingers.

Chicken "Sauce"

Serves 4–6
680 g (18 oz) chicken
2 tbsp lard
½ tbsp rice wine or sherry
2 tbsp soy sauce
1 tbsp sugar
300 ml (10 fl oz) stock
1 tbsp cornstarch
2 scallions, cut into 2.5 cm (1 in) lengths

1 Cut off the wings and parson's nose off the chicken, then chop it into about 20 pieces with the bone still attached.
2 Heat up the lard over high heat; stirfry the chicken pieces for about 30 seconds; add wine or sherry, soy sauce and sugar; stir until the chicken turns brown, then add the stock. Bring it to a boil, reduce heat to simmer for 10 minutes or until the stock is reduced by one third; now increase the heat, add the cornstarch mixed in a little water, blend well. When the juice is further reduced by half add the scallions and serve.

Cook's tip
Each chicken piece should be wrapped in a dark, sauce, hence the name of this dish.

Chicken in Vinegar Sauce

Serves 4–6
230 g (8 oz) chicken breast
1 egg white
1 tbsp rice wine or dry sherry
1 tsp salt
1 tbsp cornstarch
90 g (3 oz) bamboo shoots
3–4 dried red chilies, soaked
3 tbsp oil

Vinegar Sauce
1 slice fresh ginger, peeled and finely chopped
1 clove garlic, finely chopped
1 scallion, finely chopped
1 tbsp vinegar
1 tbsp soy sauce
1 tbsp sugar
3 tbsp stock
1 tbsp cornstarch

1 Score the skinless surface of the chicken in a criss-cross pattern; cut it into oblong pieces about the size of a stamp. Marinate it with the egg white, wine or sherry, salt and cornstarch.
2 Cut the bamboo shoots to roughly the same size as the chicken; finely chop the soaked red chilies.
3 Finely chop the fresh ginger, garlic and scallion; mix the sauce in a bowl.
4 Warm up the oil and stirfry the chicken pieces for about 2 minutes; add chilies and bamboo shoots, stir a few more times then add the sauce. Blend well; serve as soon as the sauce thickens.

Chicken Fu-yung

Serves 4–6
4 chicken breasts
4 tbsp chicken stock
6 egg whites
1 tbsp cornstarch
1 tsp salt
240 ml (8 fl oz) peanut oil
2 slices fresh ginger
1 clove garlic
2 tsp ham, ground
2 tsp fresh cilantro leaves, finely chopped

Sauce
60 ml (2 fl oz) chicken stock
½ tsp salt
1 tbsp cornstarch
2 tsp Chinese yellow wine

1 Pound the chicken breasts with the back of a cleaver and grind the chicken meat finely. Add 2 tbsp chicken stock to the meat and force the mixture through a sieve. Add 1 tbsp egg white to the strained meat and stir well.

2 Blend 1 tbsp cornstarch with 2 tbsp chicken stock. Mix the egg whites, salt and ground chicken together, stirring with a fork in one direction only, and add the blended cornstarch, continuing to stir and mix the ingredients thoroughly.

3 Heat a pan until it is very hot and add the peanut oil. When the oil is warm, add tablespoonfuls of the egg white and ground chicken mixture. Reduce the heat to low and use a spatula to push the egg mixture back and forth in the saucepan. When it begins to set into snowflake-like pieces, remove them with a slotted spoon, drain and set them aside on a plate to keep warm.

4 Heat 2 tbsp oil in the saucepan. Add the ginger and garlic, but remove and discard them when they have turned brown.

5 Blend together the ingredients for the sauce, add to the saucepan and bring to a boil. Stir and pour over the egg-white mixture.

6 Sprinkle the ground ham over the sauce and garnish with the chopped cilantro leaves before serving.

Kung-po Style Chicken

Serves 4–6

560 g (4 oz) chicken breast
4 tbsp peanut oil
1 tsp peppercorns
1 tsp dried red chili, sliced
1 tsp Chinese yellow wine or dry sherry
3 slices fresh ginger
1 tsp garlic, chopped
2 tsp scallions, chopped
110 g (4 oz) roasted peanuts

Seasoning	**Sauce**
1 tsp sugar	1 tsp sugar
1 tbsp dark	2 tsp vinegar
soy sauce	1 tbsp dark
1 tbsp cornstarch	soy sauce
	3 tbsp stock
	2 tsp cornstarch

1 Cut the chicken into 1.25 cm (½ in) cubes and mix the meat with the seasoning ingredients.
2 In a separate bowl, blend together the ingredients for the sauce and set aside.
3 Heat the oil in a saucepan, add the peppercorns and dried red chilies and when the chilies darken in color, pour the oil into a bowl through a strainer. Discard the peppercorns.
4 Return the oil and the dried red chilies to the saucepan, and add the chicken. Stirfry for 1 minute, add the yellow wine, then the ginger, garlic and scallions. Keep on stirring and turning the ingredients. Add the sauce ingredients, stir well, then add the roast peanuts. Stir and serve.

Steamed Chicken

Serves 4–6

900 g (2 lb) young chicken
4–5 Chinese dried mushrooms
90 g (3 oz) bamboo shoots
60 g (2 oz) cooked ham
90 g (3 oz) broccoli stalks
2 scallions
2 slices fresh ginger, peeled
3 tbsp rice wine or sherry
1 tsp salt
500 ml (17 fl oz) clear stock
2 tbsp soy sauce

1 Clean the chicken thoroughly; place it in a large pot, cover with cold water and boil for 25 minutes. Remove and cool it in cold water, then carefully remove the meat from the bones and carcass (but keep the skin on). Cut the meat into thin slices the size of a matchstick.

2 Soak the mushrooms in warm water for about 20 minutes, squeeze dry and discard the hard stalks, then cut them into slices as well. Cut the bamboo shoots and ham into pieces the same size as the chicken. Split the broccoli stalks in half lengthways, cut them into 24 sticks, parboil for a few minutes and drain.

3 Place the bamboo shoots, mushrooms and ham slices in alternating rows in the bottom of a large bowl and arrange the chicken pieces on top with the skin side down. Place the broccoli stalks all around the chicken with the crushed carcass in the middle, add scallions cut into short lengths, fresh ginger, 1½ tbsp rice wine or sherry, ½ tsp salt, 360 ml (12 fl oz) stock and steam vigorously for 30 minutes. Remove and discard the scallions and fresh ginger, then pour the contents of the bowl into a large serving dish.

4 Heat up the remaining stock with the stock in which the chicken has been steamed and add soy sauce, the remaining salt and rice wine or sherry. When it starts to boil, skim off any scum; pour the stock over the chicken and serve.

Steamed Chicken with Chinese Mushrooms

Serves 4–6
450 g (1 lb) chicken breast and thigh meat
1 tsp salt
½ tsp monosodium glutamate
1 tbsp red wine or sherry
1 tsp sugar
1 tsp cornstarch
3–4 Chinese dried mushrooms, soaked
2 slices fresh ginger, peeled
freshly ground Sichuan pepper
1 tsp sesame oil or lard

1 Cut the chicken breasts and thighs into small pieces and mix with salt, monosodium glutamate, rice wine or sherry, sugar and cornstarch.
2 Thinly shred the mushrooms and fresh ginger.
3 Grease a heatproof plate with a little oil or lard, place the chicken pieces on it with the mushrooms and fresh ginger shreds on top, add ground pepper and all the sesame oil.
4 Steam vigorously for 20 minutes. Serve hot.

Oil-braised Chicken

Serves 4–6

560 g (14 oz) young chicken
2 tbsp soy sauce
2 tbsp rice wine or sherry
½ tsp five-spice powder
2 scallions, finely chopped
1 slice fresh ginger, peeled and finely chopped
oil for deep frying

Dipping Sauce

chili sauce
Sichuan peppercorns, crushed

1 Chop the chicken down the middle into two halves.
   Marinate with soy sauce, the wine or sherry,
   five-spice powder, finely chopped scallions and
   fresh ginger. After 20–30 minutes, take the chicken
   halves out and pat them dry with paper towels.

2 Heat up the oil in a deep fryer and, before the oil
   gets too hot, deep fry the halves for about
   5 minutes or until they start to turn golden, then
   take them out. Wait for the oil to get really hot,
   then fry the halves again until brown, take them
   out and chop them into small pieces; arrange
   on a plate.

3 Heat up the marinade; let it bubble for a while
   then pour it all over the chicken. Serve with chili
   sauce and Sichuan pepper as a dip.

Salted Chicken

Serves 4–6

900 g (2 lb) young chicken
2 tbsp soy sauce
4 slices fresh ginger, peeled
4 scallions
2 star anise
½ tbsp salt
4 tbsp *mei kuei lu chiew* (rose-petal wine)
   or fruit-based brandy
3.25 kg (185 oz) kosher salt
stock (for the dip)

1 Clean the chicken; blanch for a short while in
   boiling water. Remove and coat the whole chicken
   with soy sauce, then hang it up to dry.

2 Finely chop 2 slices fresh ginger and 2 scallions,
   crush the star anise; mix them with ½ tbsp salt
   and *mei kuei lu chiew*, and place this "marinade"
   inside the chicken. Wrap it in a large sheet of foil.

3 In a large casserole dish in the oven, heat the
   kosher salt for a few minutes and remove from
   the oven. Make a hole in the middle of the salt
   and place the foil-wrapped chicken in it. Cover
   the chicken with more salt so that it is completely
   buried. Return to the oven for 15 minutes. Remove
   the chicken, and take it out of the foil, checking it
   is cooked through (the salt can be kept for further
   use). Chop it into small pieces and arrange on a
   serving dish.

4 Finely chop the remaining fresh ginger and
   scallions; mix with a little salt and stock as a dip.

Crispy "Five-Spiced" Chicken Legs

Serves 4–6

8 chicken drumsticks
2½ tsp salt
pepper to taste
1 tsp ground ginger
vegetable oil for
    deep frying

Sauce

300 ml (10 fl oz)
    good stock
1½ tbsp hoisin sauce
1½ tbsp yellow
    bean paste
1 tsp pepper
1½ tbsp mixed
    five-spice powder

1   Rub the chicken drumsticks with a mixture of the salt, pepper and ground ginger. Leave to season for 30 minutes. Bring a saucepan of water to a boil, add the drumsticks and cook for 3 minutes. Drain and cool.

2   Place the sauce ingredients in a wok or saucepan and bring to a boil. Add the drumsticks and simmer for about 15 minutes. Leave the drumsticks to cool in the sauce for 15 minutes, then remove and drain thoroughly. Heat the oil in a wok or deep fryer. When hot, gently fry the chicken for about 5 minutes until golden brown.

3   Remove the knuckle from the drumstick and put a cutlet frill on the exposed bone. Arrange on a heated plate and serve.

Chicken, Mushrooms and Bamboo Shoots

Serves 4–6

230 g (8 oz) chicken breast
½ tsp salt
1 egg white
2 tsp cornstarch
90 g (3 oz) bamboo shoots
3 dried Chinese mushrooms, soaked
½ red pepper
1 carrot
2 scallions
1 tsp crushed peanuts to garnish

Sauce

1 tbsp soy sauce
1 tbsp sugar
1 tbsp vinegar
1½ tbsp cornstarch
2 tbsp water

1 Cut the chicken into small slices not much bigger than a postage stamp; mix with salt, egg white and cornstarch.
2 Slice the bamboo shoots, mushrooms, red pepper and carrots; cut the scallions into short lengths; mix the sauce in a bowl.
3 Heat up the oil, stirfry the chicken until its color changes; scoop out with a slotted spoon. Toss the bamboo shoots, mushrooms and carrots into the wok, stir a few times; put the chicken back, stir a few more times. Add the sauce with the crushed peanuts, blend well. As soon as the sauce thickens, dish out and serve.

Chicken and Cashew Nuts

Serves 4–6

300 g (10 oz) chicken breast, sliced	2 tbsp oyster sauce
flour	1 tbsp light soy sauce
100 g (3½ oz) scallion with white part cut into 5 cm (2 in) pieces	2 cloves garlic, chopped
	25 g (1 oz) cashew nuts, roasted
3 tbsp peanut oil	1 tbsp sugar
4 pieces dried red chili, fried and sliced	few drops dark soy sauce
	75 g (3 oz) onion, sliced

1 Flour chicken and fry in oil.
2 Remove from pan. Put the chili and the garlic into the oil before adding the rest of the ingredients.
3 Fry until cooked, serve with rice.

Chicken in Yellow Bean Sauce

Serves 4–6
230 g (8 oz) chicken breast
1 egg white
2 tsp cornstarch
vegetable oil for deep frying
2 tbsp lard
2 tbsp crushed yellow bean sauce
1 tsp sugar
1 tbsp rice wine or sherry
1 slice fresh ginger, peeled and finely chopped

1   Soak the chicken meat in cold water for 1 hour, separate the meat from the white tendon and membrane, then dice it into 1¾ cm (⅓ in) cubes. Mix it with the egg white and cornstarch together with a little water—around 2 tsp.
2   Heat the oil in a deep fryer, lower the chicken cubes in and separate them with chopsticks or a fork. As soon as they start to turn golden, scoop them out with a slotted spoon and drain.
3   Meanwhile heat the lard in a wok or frying pan, add the crushed bean sauce, stir until the sizzling noise dies down then add the sugar followed by wine or sherry and finely chopped fresh ginger. After about 10–15 seconds, it should have a smooth consistency. Now add the chicken cubes and stir well for 5 seconds so that each cube is coated with this bright reddish sauce. Serve.
4   This is a very popular dish, usually served during the early stages of a banquet.

Chicken Casserole

Serves 4–6
1–1.3 kg (2½–3 lb) chicken
1 tbsp five-spice powder
2 tbsp sugar
600 ml (1 pt) soy sauce
1 slice fresh ginger
1 scallion
Vegetable oil for deep frying

1   Wash and dry the chicken thoroughly. Put the five-spice powder into a large pot or casserole dish, add sugar, soy sauce and about 240 ml (8 fl oz) water. Bring it to a boil, then reduce the heat and simmer until it turns dark brown.
2   Parboil the chicken for 2 to 3 minutes, then place it in another pot of clean boiling water; add the fresh ginger and scallion; cook for about 40 minutes over gentle heat; remove and let it cool for a short while.
3   Cook the chicken in the sauce (prepared in step 1) for about 15 minutes, turning it over once or twice so that the entire chicken becomes dark red. Remove the meat from the sauce and drain.
4   Heat the oil over a high heat until smoking, then fry the chicken for about 15 minutes until the skin becomes dark brown but not quite burnt; remove. Chop up the chicken with a sharp cleaver and arrange it neatly on a plate and serve.

Stirfried Chicken with Peppers

Serves 4–6

230 g (8 oz) chicken breast
1½ tsp salt
1 egg white
1½ tbsp cornstarch
2 scallions
1 small green pepper
1 small red pepper
vegetable oil for deep frying
3 tbsp stock
1 tbsp rice wine or sherry

1 Cut the chicken into 2.5 cm (1 in) pieces, mix them with a little salt, the egg white and 1 tbsp cornstarch, in that order (this is very important).
2 Cut the scallions and peppers to the same size as the chicken.
3 Deep fry the chicken cubes on medium heat for only a few seconds; scoop out and drain.
4 Pour off the excess oil, leaving about 1 tbsp in the wok; put in the scallions and peppers; stir and add the stock, wine or sherry, the remaining salt and cornstarch; mix well then add the chicken cubes; blend together and serve.

Spicy Stirfried Chicken

Serves 4–6

900 g (2 lb) chicken
3–4 dried red chilies
2–3 Chinese dried mushrooms, soaked
2 slices fresh ginger, peeled
2 scallions
½ tsp Sichuan peppercorns
3 tbsp oil
2 tsp salt
1 tbsp light soy sauce
1 tbsp vinegar
1 tbsp *Kaoliang* spirit
1 tbsp cornstarch
1 tsp sesame oil

1 Plunge the chicken into a pot of boiling water for 10 minutes, then rinse it in cold water and leave it to cool. Take the meat off the bone, and cut it into 2.5 x 1.25 cm (1 x ½ in) strips.
2 Cut the mushrooms, dried red chilies, fresh ginger and scallions into shreds, and crush the peppercorns.
3 Warm up the oil, first put in the chilies, fresh ginger, scallions and pepper, then add the chicken and mushrooms, stir for a few seconds. Now add salt, soy sauce, vinegar and *Kaoliang*; when the juice starts to bubble, add the cornstarch mixed with a little water. Blend well; adding the sesame oil just before serving.

Chicken with Mixed Peppers

Serves 4

60 ml (2 fl oz) peanut oil
2 cloves garlic, chopped
300 g (10 oz) chicken breast, sliced
3 peppers; 1 green, 1 red and 1 yellow
1 red chili, sliced lengthwise
50 g (2 oz) onion, sliced
1 tsp fish sauce
½ tbsp light soy sauce
¼ tsp dark soy sauce
1 tbsp oyster sauce
50 g (2 oz) fresh basil

1 Chop the peppers. Heat oil in wok or large frying pan, add the garlic and chicken. Fry well and add the peppers and chili.
2 Add the onion, and then one by one add the rest of the ingredients, with basil last.
3 Remove from heat immediately and serve with rice.

Beijing Duck and Wraps

Serves 6–8
2.25–2.75 kg (5–6 lb) duck
40–50 Wraps (see opposite)
6 scallions
½ cucumber, halved and seeded
1–2 red chilies

Coating
1 tbsp sugar, honey
  or cornsyrup
1 tsp cornstarch
½ tsp vinegar

Sauce
2 tbsp hoisin sauce
1 tbsp peanut butter
1 tbsp sesame oil
1 tbsp Chinese
  yellow wine

Wraps (makes about 40)
510 g (20 oz) all-purpose flour
360 ml (12 fl oz) boiling water
1 tbsp sesame oil

For the duck

1 Clean the duck, removing and discarding any excess fat in the cavity. Tie a piece of string around its neck. Pat dry.
2 Bring 1.25 litres (2½ pt) water to a boil and turn off the heat. Put the duck into the water and turn it backwards and forwards for about 1 minute. Remove. Bring the water to a boil again and repeat the previous step. Do this twice more (four times in all).
3 Hang the duck in a cool, draughty place for about 5 hours.
4 Mix the coating ingredients with 180 ml (6 fl oz) hot water and brush the duck all over with the mixture. Hang to dry for a further 4 hours and apply a second coat.
5 Preheat the oven to 230°C/450°F/Gas Mark 8. Put a roasting pan in the oven with a wire rack in it, making sure there is a space of about 5 cm (2 in) between the rack and the pan.
6 Place the duck on the rack, breast side up, and roast for 8 minutes. Turn the duck over using a towel—not a fork—and roast for 8 minutes more.
7 Reduce the temperature to 180°C/350°F/Gas Mark 4 and turn the duck breast side up again. Roast for 20 minutes. Lower the temperature to 120°C/250°F/Gas Mark ½ and roast for 10 minutes. Increase the heat again to 230°C/450°F/ Gas Mark 8 and roast the duck for about 10 minutes. At this point you have to watch carefully to make sure that the skin does not burn. Turn off the heat once the skin has turned a rich deep red.
8 While the duck is roasting prepare the wraps (opposite).

Wraps

1. Place the unsifted flour in a mixing bowl. Make a well in the center and add a boiling water, stirring rapidly with a fork.
2. Knead the dough well on a lightly floured surface until it is smooth and firm. Return the dough to the mixing bowl, cover and leave to stand for 1 hour.
3. Knead the dough briefly on a lightly floured surface and roll into a sausage 4 cm (1½ in) in diameter. Pull it apart with your fingers to make about 40 equal-sized pieces. Roll the pieces between your hands to make smooth balls, making sure they are all the same size.
4. Lightly oil the fingers and palms of your hands and flatten each ball until it is 6 mm (¼ in) thick. Brush the top with sesame oil.
5. Place one piece of dough on top of another, oiled sides facing, and roll out into a flat pancake about 12–17 cm (5–7 in) across.
6. Heat the frying pan and brush the bottom with sesame oil. Add the paired wraps to the frying pan one at a time. Cook over a medium heat for 30 seconds, turn and cook the other side for 30 seconds.
7. Pull the paired wraps apart with your fingers to make two thin wraps. Place them on a large piece of foil, one on top of the other, oiled side up.
8. Wrap them in the foil and steam for 30 minutes. Serve as an accompaniment to Beijing Duck (see opposite page). Any leftover wraps can be wrapped in foil and kept in the fridge for up to 3 days.

To Serve

1. Cut the scallions into 5 cm (2in) lengths, shred the tip of each piece and put it in iced water for 10 minutes. Cut the cucumber into similar lengths. Decorate each piece with a red chili slice if desired.
2. Blend the sauce ingredients over low heat. Remove the skin from the duck. Hold the knife horizontally and carve the meat from the breast and legs, cutting at an angle of 15 degrees. Arrange the skin and meat separately on a large plate and serve it with wraps, scallions and cucumber and the sauce.
3. Diners help themselves. They place one wrap flat on a plate, put a piece of duck in the center, dip a scallion in the sauce and put it on top of the duck, wrap it up and eat it.

Aromatic Crispy Duck

Serves 6–8

1.75–2.25 kg (4–5 lb) duck
vegetable oil for deep frying

Cooking Sauce

1.5 l (3 pts) good stock
6 tbsp sugar
6 slices fresh ginger
10 tbsp soy sauce
4 tbsp yellow bean paste
6 tbsp rice wine or dry sherry
6 pieces star anise
½ tsp five-spice powder
¼ tsp pepper

1 Mix the ingredients for the cooking sauce in a large saucepan. Clean the duck thoroughly and cut in half down the backbone. Place into the liquid and submerge.

2 Simmer the duck gently for 2 hours. Remove from the cooking liquid and leave to cool. When required, heat the oil in a wok or deep fryer. When hot, place the duck gently in the oil and fry for 10–11 minutes. Drain well and serve.

Duck with Rice

Serves 4

1 roasted duck (rub with red food
   coloring before roasting), boned
   and cut into 6.5 x 1.25 cm
   (2½ x ½ in) slices
630 g (20 oz) cooked rice
4 tbsp thinly sliced pickled fresh ginger
4 tbsp thinly sliced sweet dill pickle

Cooked Sauce

500 ml (17 fl oz) chicken stock
1 tbsp sugar
½ tbsp light soy sauce
¼ tbsp dark soy sauce
1 tsp flour

Soy Chili Sauce

120 ml (4 fl oz) dark soy sauce
3 fresh red chilies, sliced thinly
1 tbsp sugar
½ tbsp vinegar

1   Heat the ingredients for the cooked sauce
    in a saucepan and boil for 1 minute. Mix the
    ingredients for the soy chili sauce in a bowl and
    put aside.
2   Warm the duck and rice at 180°C/350°F/Gas
    Mark 4 for 5 minutes. Then, divide the rice
    between four serving plates, and arrange the duck
    meat on top. Spoon the cooked sauce on top of
    each, and place ginger and pickle slices around
    the edges. Serve with the soy chili sauce on the
    side.

Stirfried Shredded Duck and Beansprouts

Serves 4–6

340 g (12 oz) roast duck meat from the back of
   Beijing Duck (see page 32)
4–6 medium dried black mushrooms
3 tbsp peanut oil
2 tsp chopped fresh ginger
1½ tsp garlic, chopped
560 g (14 oz) beansprouts
1 tsp Chinese yellow wine

Sauce

1 tsp salt
1 tbsp light soy sauce
1 tsp sesame oil
1 tsp sugar
1 tbsp cornstarch
4 tbsp stock
2–3 tbsp peanut oil

1   Shred the roast duck meat.
2   Soak the black mushrooms in hot water for
    30 minutes. Remove and discard the stems
    and shred the caps.
3   Heat 1 tbsp oil in a saucepan over high heat
    and add 1 tsp chopped ginger and ¾ tsp
    chopped garlic.
4   Add the beansprouts, stirfrying over very high heat
    for 1 minute. Remove and set aside.
5   Heat 2 tbsp oil in the saucepan. Add the
    remaining ginger, garlic and the black mushroom
    shreds. Stirfry for 30 seconds, add the roast duck
    and beansprouts. Stirfry briefly. Add the sauce
    ingredients and stir rapidly over a very high heat
    for 30 seconds. Sprinkle with 1 tsp Chinese yellow
    wine and serve.

Braised Four Treasures

Serves 4–6
6 duck feet
4 duck wings
10 duck tongues
5–6 duck kidneys
2 tbsp dark soy sauce
240 ml (8 fl oz) lard for deep frying
1 scallion, finely chopped
1 slice fresh ginger, finely chopped
300 ml (10 fl oz) chicken stock
2 tbsp rice wine or dry sherry
½ tsp monosodium glutamate (optional)
1 tbsp crushed bean sauce

1 Clean the feet in warm water and remove the outer skin, then parboil for 20 minutes. Cool them in cold water and cut into small pieces about 1.25 cm (½ in) in length.
2 Parboil the wings for 20 minutes. Cool them in cold water and cut into small pieces similar to the webs.
3 Clean the tongues in warm water and remove the outer layer of skin; parboil for 10 minutes, then cool in cold water.
4 Parboil the kidneys for 15 minutes and remove the outer layer of fat. Split each in half, cut each half in two, then marinate in a little soy sauce. Heat the lard in a wok or saucepan until smoking; fry the kidney pieces for 5 minutes or until golden, then remove and drain.
5 Leaving about 2 tbsp of lard in the saucepan, first fry the finely chopped scallion and fresh ginger; add the chicken stock with wine or sherry, monosodium glutamate (if using), crushed bean sauce and the remaining soy sauce, stir and add the "four treasures". Bring to a boil, then reduce the heat and simmer for about 15 minutes. When the stock is reduced by half, increase the heat to high to thicken the gravy, and serve.

Braised Duck

Serves 4–6
60 ml (2 fl oz) dark soy sauce
1 tsp salt
5½ tbsp red yeast rice (available from Chinese grocery stores)
2 tbsp rice wine or sherry
5½ tbsp granulated sugar, crushed
2 tsp Chinese cinnamon bark (available at Chinese grocery stores)
1 tsp fennel seeds
2 scallions
2 slices fresh ginger
2 kg (48 oz) duck
5½ tbsp sugar
1½ tbsp cornstarch

1 Clean the duck thoroughly; place it in a large pot with its back facing upwards; add enough water to cover it.
2 Add the red yeast rice, soy sauce, salt, rice wine or sherry, sugar, cinnamon bark, fennel seeds, scallions and fresh ginger. Bring it to a rapid boil and keep the heat fairly high for 1 hour
3 After 1 hour turn the duck over and simmer gently for ½ hour; take it out to cool.
4 Leave about half the juice in the pot and add the sugar and when it is dissolved pour through a strainer to get rid of the spices.
5 Mix the cornstarch with a little cold water to thicken the gravy, then leave to cool. Chop the duck into small pieces, pour the gravy over it and serve.

Cantonese Roast Duck

Serves 4–6

2–2.25 kg (4½–5 lb) duck
1 tsp salt

Stuffing

2 tbsp sugar	½ tsp five-spice
2 tbsp rice wine	powder
(or sherry)	2 slices fresh ginger,
1 tbsp yellow bean	peeled
sauce	2 scallions
1 tbsp hoisin sauce	1 tbsp oil

Coating

4 tbsp honey	1 tbsp vinegar
1 tsp "red powder"	360 ml (12 fl oz) water
(or food coloring)	

1 Clean the duck well; pat it dry with a cloth or paper towels inside and out. Rub both inside and out with salt, then tie the neck tightly with string so that no liquid will drip out when it is hanging head down.

2 Heat the oil in a saucepan, mix in the sugar, rice wine or sherry, bean sauce and hoisin sauce, five-spice powder and finely chopped ginger and scallions. Bring it to a boil, pour it into the cavity of the duck and sew it up securely.

3 Plunge the whole duck into a large pot of boiling water for a few seconds only; take it out and baste it thoroughly with the "coating" mixture then hang it up to dry for at least 4–5 hours, or ideally overnight, in a well-ventilated place.

4 Roast the duck in a moderately hot oven— 200°C/400°F/Gas Mark 6—hanging on a meat hook with its head down; place a tray of cold water in the bottom of the oven to catch the drippings. After 25 minutes or so, reduce the heat to 180°C/350°F/Gas Mark 4 roast for 30 minutes more, basting once or twice during the cooking with the remaining coating mixture. When it is done, let it cool for a while, then remove the strings and pour the liquid stuffing out. Use as the sauce when serving the duck.

Soy Braised Duck

Serves 4–6

1.5 kg (38 oz) duck
3 tbsp rice wine or sherry
oil for deep frying
60 g (2 oz) sliced carrots
2 slices fresh ginger, peeled and crushed
2 scallions, cut into short lengths
2 tbsp hoisin sauce
1 tbsp sugar
3 tbsp soy sauce
2 tbsp wood ear mushrooms, soaked
2 tbsp sliced bamboo shoots
seasonal greens to serve

1 Clean and parboil the duck, then rub it all over with rice wine or sherry.

2 Heat the oil and deep fry the duck until golden; remove, chop it into half lengthways.

3 Pour off the excess oil, leaving about 2 tbsp in the wok; add the ginger, scallions, wood ear mushrooms, bamboo shoots, hoisin sauce, sugar, and soy sauce. Turn it over once or twice to cover it with the sauce. Take the duck out; place it on a plate and steam vigorously for 1–2 hours. Serve with seasonal greens.

Tea-smoked Duck

Serves 4–6
1.5–1.75 kg (3½–4 lb) duck

Marinade
½ tbsp salt
2 Sichuan peppercorns
½ tsp ground pepper
3 tbsp rice wine or sherry
2 tbsp hoisin sauce

Smoking Materials
60 g (2 oz) tea leaves
60 g (2 oz) camphor leaves
110 g (4 oz) sawdust
110 g (4 oz) cypress tree branch
oil for deep frying

1 Make the marinade; rub it all over the duck both inside and out; leave to marinate for 12 hours, then let it dry in an airy place.

2 Mix the smoking materials together, then divide into three portions and put one portion in an earthenware bowl; place the bowl inside a large container such as a wine barrel sawn in half. Light a piece of charcoal until red; put it inside the bowl and place a sheet of wire netting on top. Lay the duck on the wire netting and place the other half of the wine barrel on top so that it keeps the smoke in. After 10 minutes, add the second portion of the smoking material to the bowl together with a new piece of burning charcoal, then turn the duck over and replace the lid. After 7 minutes add the last portion of the smoking material with another piece of burning charcoal, turn the duck over again and smoke for another 5 minutes. The duck should be nice and brown all over.

Oil-soaked Duck

Serves 4–6
1–1.5 kg (3–38 oz) duck
3 tbsp rice wine or sherry
3½ tbsp sugar
6 tbsp stock
3 tbsp soy sauce
few fennel seeds
1 slice fresh ginger
oil for deep frying
5 tbsp orange juice

Garnish
2 tomatoes
6 scallions, white parts only
230 g (8 oz) Chinese pickled turnip or radish

1 Clean the duck; discard the pinions (wing tips); blanch in a large pot of boiling water; place it on a long dish, stomach side up. Mix 2 tbsp rice wine or sherry with 2 tbsp sugar, stock, soy sauce, fennel seeds and fresh ginger; pour it all over the duck; steam vigorously for 15 minutes. Pierce the stomach with a sharp-pointed chopstick or knitting needle a dozen times or so; turn the bird over, steam for another 15 minutes, then turn it over once more and steam for 15 minutes more. Now deep fry it in hot oil until dark brown. Remove.

2 Pour off the excess oil, put in the remaining rice wine or sherry, sugar, orange juice and about one-third of the juice from the duck. Add the duck; turn it around a few times to make sure that it is well coated, then remove and chop it into small pieces. On a serving plate, rearrange it in the shape of the original duck; pour the juice over it.

3 Serve it with sliced tomato, grated scallions and pickled turnip or radish. You can make your own pickle as follows: Cut some turnip or radish into thin slices; marinate with a little salt for a while, squeeze out the liquid, then in a jar mix it with sugar and vinegar and leave for several hours.

Smoked Duck, Sichuan Style

Serves 4–6
900 g (2 lb) duck
1½ tsp peppercorns
2 tbsp salt
2 tbsp jasmine tea
1 tbsp sugar
½ tsp chili powder
2 tbsp Chinese yellow wine or dry sherry
peanut oil for deep frying
1 tbsp sesame oil

1 Clean the duck and cover it with water, add peppercorns and salt leave for 4 hours.

2 Blanch the duck in boiling water for 5 minutes. Dry thoroughly.

3 Heat a dry saucepan over moderate heat, add the jasmine tea and sugar and cover with a lid. After 1 minute, place a wire rack in the saucepan and lay the duck on the rack. Replace the lid firmly and smoke the duck for about 10 minutes over low heat and then leave to stand in the smoke until it turns light golden brown.

4 Rub the duck all over with chili powder and Chinese yellow wine and steam for 2 hours. Set aside.

5 Heat the peanut oil in a deep saucepan. When hot, add the duck and deep fry until the skin is rich golden brown in color and crispy.

6 Take the duck out of the saucepan and brush with sesame oil. Chop into bite-sized pieces and serve.

Red Duck Curry

Serves 4-6

500 ml (1 pt) coconut milk
1 roast duck, de-boned and sliced, skin on
15 cherry tomatoes
5 pieces fresh large red chilies,
   sliced in half lengthways
3 kaffir lime leaves, chopped
2 tbsp fish sauce
1 tsp salt
3 tbsp sugar
   100 g (4 oz) fresh basil

Curry Paste

7 dried red chilies
1 tsp cilantro, chopped
4 garlic cloves, chopped
1 lemon grass, sliced
1 tbsp shrimp paste
25 g (1 oz) galangal, chopped
1 tsp cracked white pepper
1 tsp kaffir lime leaves, chopped
½ tsp cilantro seeds

1 To make the curry paste, pound all the ingredients into a fine paste with a pestle and mortar or electronic blender.

2 To make the curry, add the coconut milk to a wok or large saucepan and heat. Then add the curry paste and fry together for 5 minutes.

3 Add the rest of the coconut milk, boil, then add the duck, cherry tomatoes and red chili. Boil, then add the rest of the ingredients and boil for 5 minutes more and serve with rice.

Sunflower Duck

Serves 4–6
1.75 kg (4 lb) duck
30 g (1 oz) Chinese dried mushrooms
110 g (4 oz) cooked ham
300 ml (10 fl oz) good chicken or duck stock
2 tbsp dark soy sauce
1 tbsp sugar
1 tsp salt

1 Clean the duck inside and out, then split it down the middle lengthwise with a cleaver. Place the two halves on a plate, skin side down, and steam vigorously for 2–3 hours. Remove and leave it to cool for a while with the skin side up.

2 Soak the mushrooms in warm water for 10 minutes, discard the stalks and cut the large ones into two to three pieces. Cut the ham into thin slices about the size of a matchbox.

3 Cut off the neck and wings of the duck, then very carefully remove the meat from the carcass and bones. Cut the meat into thin slices and neatly arrange them on a plate in the shape of the duck with the skin side up, alternately overlapping each piece of meat with a piece of mushroom and a slice of ham. Then very carefully turn the meat out into a large, deep dish or bowl, pour over about a third of the chicken/duck stock and add soy sauce, sugar and salt and steam vigorously for about 20 minutes, then place it back onto the plate and rearrange if necessary.

Roast Goose

Serves 6–8
2.75 kg (6 lb) goose
1 tbsp soy bean paste
1 tsp five-spice powder
1 piece star anise
1 tbsp sugar
2 tbsp light soy sauce
2 tsp chopped garlic
1 tbsp Chinese yellow wine
1.5 litres (3 pt) boiling water
2 tbsp sugar
4 tbsp honey or corn syrup
4 tbsp vinegar
240 ml (8 fl oz) water

1 Cut off the feet and wing tips of the goose.

2 Blend together the soy bean paste, five-spice powder, star anise, sugar, soy sauce, chopped garlic and yellow wine and rub the mixture all over the inside of the goose. Tightly fasten the neck and tail openings with skewers or string to ensure that the mixture does not run out when the goose is hung.

3 Place the goose on a rack, breast up, and pour half a boiling water over it. Turn the goose over and pour the remaining boiling water over it. Pat the goose dry and set it aside.

4 Heat the malt sugar, honey, vinegar and water together, stirring to mix well, and brush the mixture all over the goose. Tie a piece of string around the neck of the goose and hang it up in a draughty place for 1 hour to dry.

5 Preheat the oven to 230°C/450°F/Gas Mark 8. Place the goose on a rack in a deep roasting tin and roast the goose, breast side up, for 12 minutes until golden. Turn the goose over with a towel (avoid using a fork) and roast for another 12 minutes.

6 Reduce the heat to 180°C/350°F/Gas Mark 4 and, with the goose breast side up again, roast for 20 minutes. Reduce the heat to 150°C/300°F/Gas Mark 2 and roast for 10 minutes more, then reduce the heat to 120°C/250°F/Gas Mark ½ and roast for minutes. Finally, increase the heat to 230°C/450°F/Gas Mark 8 again and roast for 10 minutes. You have to watch closely at this point to avoid burning the goose. Chop the goose into bite-sized pieces and serve.

Roast Goose Casserole with Bamboo Shoots

Serves 4–6
340 g (12 oz) Roast Goose (see page 41)
190 g (6½ oz) bamboo shoots
6 medium dried black mushrooms
small piece of dried orange peel
1 tbsp peanut oil
6 slices fresh ginger
2–3 cloves garlic, crushed
1 tbsp cornstarch
1 scallion, cut into 4¼ cm (1½ in) lengths
1 tbsp chopped fresh cilantro leaves

Sauce
1 tbsp oyster sauce
1 tbsp light soy sauce
1 tbsp dark soy sauce
½ tsp sesame oil
2 tsp Chinese yellow wine
240 ml (8 fl oz) chicken stock

1 Cut the roast goose into bite-sized pieces and the bamboo shoots into wedge shapes. Soak the black mushrooms and dried orange peel in hot water for 30 minutes. Remove and discard the mushroom stems. Finely shred orange peel. Set aside.

2 Blanch the bamboo shoots in boiling water for 5 minutes. Remove, rinse under the faucet, drain and set aside.

3 Heat the peanut oil in a casserole dish and add the ginger and garlic. When they start to smell add the roast goose, bamboo shoots, black mushrooms and orange peel, stir and cook for 1 minute.

4 Add the sauce ingredients to the saucepan and enough water to cover the ingredients. Bring to a boil, reduce the heat and simmer for 45 minutes. Thicken the sauce with 1 tbsp cornstarch mixed with an equal amount of water. Add the scallion and cilantro and serve.

MEAT

Delicious recipes for meat dishes abound all over Asia. Pork is probably the most popular since pigs are reared for their meat only and are easier to raise in those regions where cattle and sheep farming may not succeed. Nothing goes to waste, and offal is a popular ingredient in most Asian countries. Stirfrying, roasting and slow-cook methods of cooking are all popular ways to prepare meat.

Mustard and Red Chili Oil Beef with Leeks

Serves 4–6
450 g (1 lb) beef steak, rump, fillet or sirloin
1 tsp salt
1½ tbsp cornstarch
1 egg white
3 slices fresh ginger
230 g (8 oz) leeks
4 tbsp vegetable oil
30 g (1 oz) lard
1 tbsp light soy sauce
2 tbsp good stock
1 tbsp hot mustard
2 tsp red chili oil

1   Cut the beef into very thin slices and rub with salt. Toss in the cornstarch and coat in the egg white. Shred the ginger. Clean the leeks thoroughly and cut on the diagonal into 2 cm (¾ in) pieces.
2   Heat the vegetable oil in a wok or frying pan. When hot, fry half of the ginger for 30 seconds to flavor the oil. Add the leeks and stirfry for 1½ minutes. Remove and set aside. Add the lard to the saucepan. When hot, stirfry the beef for 1½ minutes. Add the soy sauce and remaining ginger, then return the leeks and stock to the saucepan. Toss together for another 30 seconds.
3   Transfer to a heated serving dish. Drizzle the mustard and chili oil evenly over the dish.

Beef and Black Mushrooms

Serves 4–6
110 g (4 oz) pork fat
560 g (1¼) lb ground beef
8 tbsp stock
1 tbsp cornstarch
1 tsp sesame oil
2½ tsp salt
12 small dried black mushrooms
1 tsp sugar
1 tbsp peanut oil

1   Cut the pork fat into tiny cubes and blanch the pieces in boiling water for 1 minute. Rinse under the faucet. Put the pork fat, beef mince, stock, cornstarch, sesame oil and 1½ tsp of salt in a mixing bowl and stir, in one direction only, with a fork until the mixture becomes sticky.
2   Soak the black mushrooms in hot water for 30 minutes, remove and discard the stems and place the caps in a bowl. Add 1 tsp salt, the sugar and peanut oil and mix well. Steam the mushrooms over medium heat for 5 minutes and set aside.
3   Divide the beef into 12 portions, molding each portion into an egg shape and place 1 mushroom on top of each "egg". Use six small dishes and place two of the beef and mushroom "eggs" in each dish. Steam over high heat for 5 minutes and serve.

Cantonese Stirfried Beef in Oyster Sauce

Serves 2

450 g (1 lb) beef steak, rump or fillet

1 tsp salt

pepper to taste

2 tbsp cornstarch

1 egg white

3 slices fresh ginger

3–4 scallions

4 tbsp vegetable oil

1 tsp lard

1½ tbsp good stock

1 tbsp soy sauce

1½ tbsp oyster sauce

1 tbsp rice wine or dry sherry

1 Cut the beef into thin strips and mix with the salt and pepper. Toss in the cornstarch and coat in the egg white. Shred the ginger. Cut the onions on the diagonal into 4 cm (1½ in) sections.

2 Heat the oil in a wok or frying pan. When hot, stirfry the ginger in the oil to flavor. Add the beef and stirfry over high heat for about 1 minute. Remove and set aside. Add the lard to the pan. When hot, stirfry the scallions for 1–2 minutes. Add the stock and soy sauce, and continue to stirfry for 30 seconds. Return the beef to the saucepan, add the oyster sauce and wine or sherry and stirfry over high heat for 30 seconds.

Stirfried Meatballs

Serves 4

450 g (1 lb) ground beef
1 egg white
4–5 tbsp water
1½ tbsp salt
1½ tbsp cornstarch
½ tbsp sesame oil
½ tsp ground pepper

1 Put all the ingredients in a mixing bowl and use a fork to stir—in one direction only—until the mixture becomes sticky and firm. Make up to 20 small meatballs, about 2 cm (¾ in) in diameter.
2 Bring about 1 l (2 pt) water to a boil, add the beef balls and remove them when they float to the surface. Set aside.
3 Follow next recipe to serve, or freeze for up to one month.

Meatball and Dried Fish Stirfry with Chinese Kale

Serves 6–8

560 g (14 oz) Meatballs (see recipe to the left)
230 g–340 g (8–12oz) dried sole
8 tbsp peanut oil
560 g (14 oz) Chinese kale
1 tsp fresh ginger, chopped
4 tbsp chicken stock
1 tbsp fish or shrimp sauce
1 tsp sugar
1 tsp garlic, chopped
2 tsp Chinese yellow wine

1 Cut about a quarter of the way through each meatball and set aside.
2 Remove the bones of the dried fish and break the flesh into bite-sized pieces. Fry the pieces in 8 tbsp oil until nicely browned. Remove, drain and set aside. Cut the kale into lengths 4 x 5 cm (1½ x 2 in).
3 Heat 3 tbsp oil in a saucepan. Add the ginger and kale, stirfrying over a very high heat for 1 minute. Add 4 tbsp chicken stock, cover and continue to cook over a very high heat for another minute.
4 Uncover the saucepan and add 1 tbsp fish or shrimp sauce and 1 tsp sugar. Stir rapidly over very high heat for 1 minute.
5 Add 2 tbsp oil, the garlic, beef balls and Chinese yellow wine, stirfrying for 2 minutes. Return the fried dried sole to the saucepan, stir for 30 seconds and serve.

Stirfried Beef, Squid, Mushrooms and Baby Corn

Serves 6–8

140 g (5 oz) filet mignon
140 g (5 oz) squid
200 g (7 oz) straw mushrooms, fresh or tinned
200 g (7 oz) baby corn
240 ml (8 fl oz) peanut oil
1 tsp salt
½ tsp garlic, crushed
3–4 slices fresh ginger
2–3 scallions, cut into 4 cm (1½ in) lengths
1½ tbsp Chinese yellow wine

Sauce

2 tsp oyster sauce
2 tsp soy sauce
½ tsp salt
1 tsp sugar
¼ tsp pepper
1 tbsp cornstarch

6 tbsp stock
few drops
  sesame oil
1 tsp Chinese
  yellow wine
4 tbsp peanut oil

Seasoning for Beef

2 tsp light soy sauce
½ tsp sesame oil
½ tsp pepper
½ tsp sugar
1 tbsp cornstarch

Seasoning for Squid

1 tsp ginger juice
  (strained from
  crushed fresh
  ginger)
1 tsp Chinese
  yellow wine
½ tsp salt
½ tsp sesame
  oil
1 tbsp cornstarch

1 Cut the beef into thin slices 5 cm x 7 cm (2 x 3 in).

2 Divide the squid into pieces 2 cm x 5 cm (¾ x 2 in), scoring the flesh on one side to form a diamond pattern. Cut the straw mushrooms and baby corn into halves.

3 Separately prepare the individual seasonings for the beef and the squid. Heat a saucepan, add the oil and heat for 1 minute over medium heat. Add the seasoned beef, stir to separate and remove with a slotted spoon after just over a minute.

4 Add the seasoned squid to the oil, removing it with a strainer when it curls up. Keep 1 tbsp oil in the saucepan. Add the baby corn, mushrooms and 1 tsp salt and stir well over high heat for 30 seconds. Remove and set aside.

5 Heat the saucepan over a very high heat and add 2 tbsp oil, the garlic and sliced ginger. When it starts to smell, add the beef, squid and onions, sprinkle 1 tbsp Chinese yellow wine over them and stir rapidly for 30 seconds. Add the baby corn and straw mushrooms. Stir for 30 seconds.

6 Blend together the sauce ingredients and add them to the pan. Stir for 10 seconds, sprinkle with ½ tbsp wine and serve.

Shredded Beef with Celery

Serves 4–6
230 g (8 oz) beef steak
60 g (2 oz) celery
45 g (1½ oz) leek or scallion
2 slices fresh ginger
3 tbsp oil
1 tbsp chili paste
2 tbsp soy sauce
½ tsp salt
1 tsp sugar
1 tbsp rice wine or sherry
1 tsp vinegar

1   Shred the beef into thin strips about the size of matches. Shred the celery and leeks to the same size (Chinese leeks are a cross between the Western leek and scallion with thin skin and green foliage). Peel the fresh ginger and cut it into thin shreds as well.

2   Heat up the wok or saucepan and put in the oil. When it starts to smoke, stirfry the beef for a short while, add the chili paste, blend well, then add the celery, leek and fresh ginger, followed by the soy sauce, salt, sugar and wine. Stirfry for 1–2 minutes, then add vinegar and serve.

Stewed Beef

Serves 4–6
2 tbsp oil
900 g (2 lb) shin of beef
3–4 scallions
2–3 slices fresh ginger
1 tsp five-spice powder
2 tbsp sugar
6 tbsp soy sauce
2 tbsp rice wine or sherry

1   This dish makes excellent use of a cheap cut of meat. It is cooked slowly so that the meat becomes really tender.

2   Cut the beef into 2.5 cm (1 in) cubes. Cut the onions into 2.5 cm (1 in) lengths.

3   Heat up the oil and brown the beef before blanching it in a pot of boiling water for a few seconds. Pour the water away and cover with fresh cold water and add scallions, fresh ginger, five-spice powder, sugar, soy sauce and rice wine or sherry, and place a tightly fitting lid over the pan. Bring it to a boil over high heat, then reduce the heat and simmer gently for 3–4 hours, after which there should be very little juice left. Serve hot or cold.

Quick-fried Beef Steak

Serves 4–6

230 g (8 oz) beef steak
1½ tbsp soy sauce
1 tbsp cornstarch
oil for deep frying
2 scallions, white parts only, cut into
   1.25 cm (½ in) lengths
2 cloves garlic, finely chopped
1 tsp vinegar
2 tsp rice wine or sherry

1 Cut the beef into thin slices and marinate with 1 tbsp soy sauce and cornstarch.
2 Heat up the oil until smoking, deep fry the beef slices for about 30 seconds only, stir with chopsticks to separate them, then quickly scoop them out with a slotted spoon.
3 Now heat up about 1 tbsp oil in a wok and toss in the onions and garlic. When they start to turn golden, put in the beef slices, add vinegar, rice wine or sherry and the remaining soy sauce, stirfry for about 30 seconds, then it is done.

Stirfried Beef with Vegetables

Serves 4–6

340 g (12 oz) beef steak
1 tbsp rice wine or sherry
1 tbsp soy sauce
1 tbsp cornstarch
oil for deep frying
90 g (3 oz) bamboo shoots
1 carrot
90 g (3 oz) broccoli
2 slices fresh ginger, peeled
3–4 Chinese dried mushrooms, soaked
1 tsp salt
3 tbsp stock

1 Cut the beef across the grain into thickish slices the size of matchboxes; mix with rice wine or sherry, soy sauce, cornstarch and a little oil; leave to marinate for 10 minutes.
2 Cut the bamboo shoots and carrot into slices the same size as the beef, cut the broccoli into small florets. Deep fry the beef in hot oil for 1½ minutes; remove and drain.
3 Pour off the excess oil, leaving about 2 tbsp oil in the wok. Wait until it smokes, toss in the fresh ginger, broccoli, bamboo shoots, carrot and mushrooms; add salt, stir a few times then add the beef with oyster sauce and stock; cook together for 1 minute. Serve hot.

Steamed Beef with Ground Rice

Serves 4–6
450 g (1 lb) beef steak
1 tbsp salted black beans, crushed
2 tbsp soy sauce
1 tbsp chili paste
1 tbsp oil
2 tbsp rice wine or sherry
2 slices fresh ginger, peeled and finely chopped
½ tsp Sichuan pepper, freshly ground
100 g (4 oz) coarsely-ground rice (use 20 per cent glutinous rice with 80 percent ordinary rice)

1 Cut the beef into 5 cm x 2 cm (2 x ¾ in) slices and 2 cm (¼ in) thick; mix with beans, soy sauce, chili paste, oil, rice wine or sherry, fresh ginger and ground pepper. Marinate for 30 minutes, then coat each piece of beef carefully with ground rice.
2 Ideally, use small dim sum bamboo steamers as seen in Cantonese restaurants, otherwise any other type of steamer will do. Steam the beef vigorously for 30 minutes (if using the tenderest rump steak, then 15 minutes will do). Serve hot.

Lamb in Sweet and Sour Sauce

Serves 4–6
230 g (8 oz) lamb fillet
1 tbsp crushed yellow bean sauce
2 slices fresh ginger, finely chopped
2 tbsp cornstarch
1½ tbsp soy sauce
1 tbsp rice wine or sherry
1 tbsp vinegar
2 tbsp sugar
oil for deep frying
½ tsp chicken fat or sesame oil

1 Thinly slice the lamb fillet and finely chop the ginger.
2 Mix the lamb with ½ tbsp cornstarch, a little water and the crushed bean sauce.
3 Mix the remaining cornstarch with soy sauce, rice wine or sherry, vinegar, sugar and the ginger.
4 Heat the oil in a wok or saucepan, fry the lamb slices for about 15 seconds and stir to separate them. When they turn pale, scoop them out and return the lamb slices to the wok over a high heat. Add the sauce mixture, stir and blend well for about 1 minute; add chicken fat or sesame oil, stir a few more times, then serve.

Aromatic Mutton

Serves 4–6
680 g (18 oz) mutton or lamb fillet
330 g (11 oz) leeks
500 ml (1 pt) peanut oil
1 tsp garlic, chopped
1 tsp Chinese yellow wine

Marinade
1 tbsp light soy sauce
1 tsp dark soy sauce
1 tsp sesame oil
2 tsp Chinese yellow wine
1 tbsp cornstarch

1 Cut the mutton fillet into thin slices. Mix together the marinade ingredients, add the mutton slices and set aside. Cut the leek into thin slices. 2 Heat a saucepan until it is very hot and add the oil. Heat the oil until it is warm and add the mutton (reserving the marinade in a separate bowl) and stir to separate. Remove, drain and set aside.

2 Heat 2 tbsp oil in the saucepan and add the chopped garlic and leek, stir and cook over very high heat for 1 minute.

3 Return the mutton to the saucepan, stirring well. Add the reserved marinade, stirring vigorously over very high heat for 15 seconds. Finally, add the Chinese yellow wine, stir for another 10 seconds and serve.

Red-cooked Lamb

Serves 4–6
680 g (18 oz) lamb fillet, in one piece
2 tbsp soy sauce
2 tbsp rice wine or sherry
1 tsp salt
½ tsp Sichuan ground pepper
1½ tbsp Chinese dried dates, soaked
125 g (4½ oz) water chestnuts, peeled
2 slices fresh ginger, peeled
2 scallions, cut into short lengths
½ tsp five-spice powder
1.8 litres (4 pt) stock
oil for deep frying
4–5 Chinese dried mushrooms, soaked
½ tsp sesame oil
1 tbsp cornstarch

1 Wash the meat thoroughly; make cuts two-thirds of the way through the meat at 1.25 cm (½ in) intervals. Blanch in boiling water for about 3 minutes; drain and coat with soy sauce.

2 Place the meat in a strainer and lower it into oil . Deep fry over moderate heat for about 1½ minutes or until it turns red; remove and drain.

3 Pour off the excess oil; put the meat back in the pan with rice wine or sherry, salt, pepper, dates, water chestnuts, fresh ginger, onions, soy sauce, five-spice powder and stock; bring to a boil, then transfer into a casserole dish. Simmer gently for 1½ hours or until the stock is reduced by half; add the mushrooms and cook for another 10 minutes. Remove the meat and cut it into 1.25 cm (½ in) pieces. Place the water chestnuts, dates and mushrooms on a serving dish with the lamb.

4 Remove the onions and fresh ginger from the gravy. Warm up 240 ml (8 fl oz) of the gravy in a small saucepan. Add sesame oil and thicken with a little cornstarch; stir to make it smooth, then pour it over the lamb and serve.

Beijing Lamb Mold

Serves 6–8

680 g (18 oz) leg
  of lamb
230 g (8 oz) pork skin
2 scallions
3 cloves garlic
3 slices fresh ginger
1½ tsp salt
pepper to taste
600 ml (1 pt) good
  stock
3 tbsp white wine
1 tbsp light soy sauce

Dipping Sauce

4 tbsp light soy sauce
1 tbsp finely chopped
  fresh ginger
1 tbsp finely
  chopped garlic
1 tbsp finely chopped
  scallion

1 Cut the lamb into 4 x 5 x 2 cm (1½ x 2 x ¾ in) pieces.
   Cut the pork skin into smaller pieces. Parboil the
   lamb and pork skin in a saucepan of water for 2
   minutes, then drain. Cut the scallions into
   4.5 cm (1¾ in) sections, keeping the green and
   white pieces separate. Thinly slice the garlic. Shred
   the ginger.

2 Place the pork skin on the bottom of a heavy
   casserole dish and cover with the lamb. Add the
   salt, pepper, white parts of the scallions and the
   ginger. Pour in the stock and about 300 ml
   (10 fl oz) water to cover the contents and bring to
   a boil. Reduce the heat to low, cover and simmer
   for 1¼ hours. Cool, then place in the fridge to
   encourage setting. The contents should be set
   after 3 hours. Remove the casserole dish from
   the fridge and peel away the pork fat and skin.
   Heat briefly to melt the preserve and then stir in
   the wine, soy sauce, garlic and green parts of the
   scallions. Pour the lamb mixture into a rectangular
   mold and leave in the fridge to set again. Mix the
   dipping sauce ingredients together. Turn the mold
   out onto a serving dish and cut into 5 mm (¼ in)
   slices. Serve with the dipping sauce.

Cassia Lamb

Serves 4–6

110 g (4 oz) lamb fillet
3 eggs
1 slice fresh ginger
2 tbsp chicken fat
1 tsp salt
½ tsp monosodium glutamate (optional)
2 tsp rice wine or dry sherry

1 Cut the lamb into thin shreds. Finely chop the fresh
   ginger. Beat the eggs and mix them with the lamb
   shreds and fresh ginger.

2 Heat the chicken fat in a wok or saucepan, put
   in the egg mixture, stir and scramble for about
   10 seconds and add salt, monosodium glutamate
   (if using) and rice wine or sherry. Stir and scramble
   for another 10 seconds. Serve.

Lamb with Mushrooms and Peppers with Crispy Rice Noodles

Serves 4–6
560 g (14 oz) lamb fillet
4 medium black mushrooms
265 g (9 oz) fresh bamboo shoots
1 green pepper
500 ml (17 fl oz) peanut oil
30 g (1 oz) dried rice vermicelli noodles
1½ tsp garlic, chopped
1½ tsp fresh ginger, chopped

Marinade
1 egg white
2 tsp cornstarch
1 tbsp light soy sauce
1 tsp sugar
1 tsp Chinese yellow wine
1 tsp sesame oil

Sauce
1 tbsp oyster sauce
1 tbsp light soy sauce
½ tsp sugar
½ tsp sesame oil
1 tbsp Chinese yellow wine
120 ml (4 fl oz) chicken stock
1 tbsp cornstarch
1 tbsp lime leaves, finely shredded
1 tbsp fresh cilantro, chopped

1 Shred the lamb into matchstick-sized pieces and mix well with the marinade. Set aside.
2 Soak the black mushrooms in hot water for 30 minutes. Cut away and discard the stems and squeeze the mushrooms to remove any excess water. Shred the caps and set aside.
3 Finely chop the bamboo shoots and green pepper. Blanch the bamboo shoots in 1 l (2 pt) boiling water for 2 minutes. Remove and rinse under faucet. Drain and set aside.
4 Heat the oil in a saucepan. Add the lamb and, after just ovcer a minute, stir to separate. Remove and set aside.
5 Add the noodles to the hot oil, removing them as soon as they fluff up (it takes only an instant). Place them as a bed on a large platter and keep warm.
6 Heat 3–4 tbsp of oil in the saucepan and add the garlic and ginger. When they start to smell, add the black mushrooms, green pepper and bamboo shoots and sauté for 1 minute. Return the lamb and stir rapidly over very high heat for 30 seconds.
7 Add the sauce ingredients and continue to stir over very high heat for another 30 seconds. Transfer to the platter and place on top of the noodles. Garnish with lime leaves and cilantro and serve.

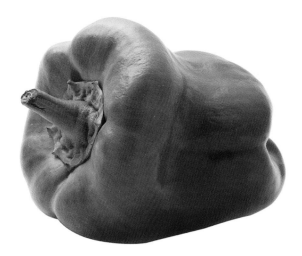

Diced Lamb with Scallions

Serves 4–6

230 g (8 oz) lamb fillet
135 g (4¾ oz) chopped scallions
1½ tbsp cornstarch
1 tsp salt
2 tsp soy sauce
1 egg white
½ tbsp rice wine or sherry
oil for deep frying
1 tsp sesame oil

1 Cut the lamb into 1.25 cm (½ in) cubes, marinate with ½ tsp salt, egg white and ¾ tbsp cornstarch. Cut the scallions into 1 cm (½ in) lengths.

2 Heat about 625 ml (1 pt) oil in a wok. Before the oil gets too hot, add the lamb cubes, separate them with chopsticks or a fork, then scoop them out and drain.

3 Pour off the excess oil and leave about 2 tbsp in the wok. Put in the scallions followed by the lamb cubes, salt, soy sauce, rice wine or sherry and the remaining cornstarch; stir for 1–2 minutes; add the sesame oil, stir a few more times, then serve.

Three-layer Shreds

Serves 4–6
50 g (2 oz) shredded cooked ham
50 g (2 oz) shredded cooked chicken meat
50 g (2 oz) shredded cooked pork (perhaps left
    over from White-cut Pork see page 57)
40 g (1½ oz) bamboo shoots
1 large Chinese dried mushroom
2 tsp salt
600 ml (1 pt) stock
½ tsp monosodium glutamate (optional)
1 tbsp lard

1　The ham, chicken, pork and bamboo shoots should be cut into matchstick-sized shreds, but keep them separate. Discard the stalk of the mushroom after soaking it in warm water for 20 minutes. Place the mushroom smooth side down in the middle of a large bowl, and arrange the ham shreds around it. Add the chicken shreds and the bamboo shoots and the pork. Spread 1 tsp salt all over it, add about 4 tbsp stock and steam vigorously for 30 minutes. Remove and turn the bowl out onto a deep serving dish.

2　Bring the remaining stock to a boil, add salt, monosodium glutamate (if using) and lard; let it bubble for a second or two then pour it all over the three-layer shreds and serve.

Mongolian Hotpot

Serves 4–6
900 g (2 lb) lamb
4 cakes tofu
4–6 Chinese dried mushrooms
560 g (14 oz) cabbage
560 g (14 oz) spinach
260 g (9 oz) transparent glass noodles

Sauce

sesame oil	fermented tofu
sesame paste	cheese
shrimp sauce	1 bundle chives,
soy sauce	chopped
Chinese yellow wine	cilantro leaves,
wine vinegar	chopped
sugar	4 scallions, chopped
chili oil	

1　Cut the lamb into wafer-thin slices and arrange the slices on a large platter (or on several smaller plates to avoid stacking up slices of lamb). Cut each cake of tofu into eight or ten pieces.

2　Put plenty of water into the hotpot. Add the mushrooms and bring to a boil.

3　Diners are encouraged to mix their own sauce. One recipe would be to mix 1 tsp each of sesame oil and sesame paste with 1 tsp each of shrimp sauce, light soy sauce, Chinese yellow wine and wine vinegar and ½ tsp sugar.

4　The more adventurous might care to add 1 tsp each of chili oil and fermented tofu cheese and chopped chives and stir in chopped cilantro and scallions.

5　Mix the sauce in a bowl, sample it and correct it to taste.

6　Pick up one or two slices of lamb at a time with chopsticks or put them in a small, long-handled wire basket, designed especially for this purpose. Cook the lamb very briefly in a boiling water in the hotpot. Transfer to the sauce bowl and eat.

7　Add the vegetables and tofu halfway through, and the bean-flour noodles towards the end, when a boiling water has turned into a rich soup after all the meat has been cooked in it.

Salt and Pepper Spareribs

Serves 4–6

290 g (10 oz) pork spareribs
1 tsp salt
1 tsp freshly ground Sichuan pepper
½ tbsp *Kaoliang* spirit
½ tsp five-spice powder
1 egg
2 tsp cornstarch
oil for deep frying

1 Chop the spareribs into small pieces; marinate with salt and pepper, *Kaoliang* spirit and five-spice powder for 15 minutes. Add egg and cornstarch and mix well.

2 Heat the oil until hot, deep fry the spareribs for 3 minutes then soak them in cold oil for 1 minute. Just before serving, crisp them in hot oil once more.

White-cut Pork

Serves 4–6

900 g (2 lb) leg of pork (skinned and de-boned)

Dipping Sauce

4 tbsp light soy sauce
1 tbsp *Kaoliang* spirit or brandy
2 scallions, finely chopped
2 slices fresh ginger, peeled and finely chopped
1 tsp sesame oil
1 tsp chili sauce (optional)
2 l (4 pt) water

1   Place the pork (in one piece, tied together with string if necessary) in a large pot; add cold water, bring it to a rapid boil; skim off the scum. Cover and simmer gently for about 1 hour. Remove from the pot and covcer; leave it to cool with the fat side up for 6–8 hours.

2   Just before serving, cut off any excess fat, leaving only a very thin layer, about 2.5 mm (1/10 in) on top, then cut the meat into small thin slices across the grain. Put any uneven bits and pieces in the center of a plate; arrange the well cut slices in two neat rows, one on each side of the pile, then neatly arrange a third row on top of the pile so that it resembles an arched bridge.

3   You can either pour the sauce mixture all over the pork and serve, or use as a dip.

Stirfried Pork, Chili and Black Olives

Serves 4–6

260 g (9 oz) pork mince
110 g (4 oz) button mushrooms
1 red chili
1 tbsp black olives in sesame oil
1 tbsp peanut oil
1 tsp garlic, chopped

Marinade

1 tsp cornstarch
2 tsp light soy sauce
1 tsp sugar
1 tsp Chinese yellow wine
2 tbsp peanut oil

1   Prepare the marinade and marinate the pork mince. Set aside. Slice the button mushrooms and finely shred the red chili. Chop the black olives into small pieces.

2   Heat 1 tbsp oil in a saucepan. Add the garlic and when it starts to smell, add the pork mince. Stir and cook over medium heat for 3 minutes. Add the black olives, button mushrooms and red chili and stirfry over medium heat for 2 minutes.

Sweet and Sour Pork

Serves 4–6

230 g (8 oz) pork, not too lean	1 egg
	½ tbsp cornstarch
90 g (3 oz) fresh bamboo shoots	2 tbsp flour
	oil for deep frying
1 green pepper	1 clove garlic
1 tsp salt	1 scallion, cut into short lengths
½ tbsp *Kaoliang* spirit	

Sauce

3 tbsp vinegar	1 tbsp soy sauce
2 tbsp sugar	½ tbsp cornstarch
½ tsp salt	1 tsp sesame oil
1 tbsp tomato paste	

1 Cut the meat into about two dozen small pieces, cut the bamboo shoots and green pepper into pieces of the same size.

2 Mix the meat pieces with salt and *Kaoliang* spirit for 15 minutes; add a beaten egg with cornstarch; blend well, then coat each piece of meat with flour.

3 Deep fry the meat in slightly hot oil for 3 minutes, then turn off the heat but leave the meat in the oil for 2 minutes; scoop out and drain. Heat up the oil again and re-fry the meat with bamboo shoots for another 2 minutes or until they are golden. Remove and drain. Pour off the excess oil, put in the garlic and green pepper followed by scallion and the sweet and sour sauce mixture; stir to make it smooth, add the meat and bamboo shoots. Serve.

Steamed Pork Liver and Sparerib of Pork

Serves 4–6
230 g (8 oz) pork liver
560 g (14 oz) sparerib of pork
1 tbsp ground bean paste
1 tbsp shallot, chopped

Marinade
1 tbsp light soy sauce
1 tsp dark soy sauce
1 tsp sesame oil
1 tsp Chinese yellow wine
1 tsp sugar
1 tbsp cornstarch

1 Cut the pork liver into slices ¾ cm (⅛ in) thick, soak the pieces in water and set aside. Chop the sparerib into bite-sized pieces. Blend together the ingredients for the marinade and add three-quarters of the mixture to the sparerib and the remaining quarter to the liver. Add the bean paste and chopped shallot to the spare rib and mix well. Lay the sparerib pieces in the bottoms of small dishes and place two or three pieces of liver on top.
2 Bring 3.75 litres (8 pt) water to a boil in a large wok with a bamboo steamer in it. Put the small dishes of sparerib and liver in the steamer, cover and steam over high heat for 12–15 minutes. Serve.

Lion's Head (Pork Meatballs with Cabbage)

Serves 4
460 g (2 oz) water chestnuts, peeled
2 tbsp dried shrimps, soaked
2 scallions
1 slice fresh ginger
50 g (1 lb) pork mince, not too lean
1 tsp salt
2 tbsp rice wine or dry sherry
½ tbsp sugar
2 tbsp light soy sauce
450 g (1 lb) Chinese cabbage
3 tbsp oil
240 ml (9 fl oz) stock

1 Finely chop the water chestnuts, shrimps, scallions and fresh ginger. Mix them together well with the pork; add salt, wine or sherry, sugar and soy sauce. Shape the meat mixture into four round balls.
2 Wash and cut the cabbage into quarters lengthways. Heat oil until smoking; stirfry the cabbage until soft, then place the meatballs on top; add stock, bring to a boil and simmer with a lid on for 20–30 minutes.
3 When serving make sure the meatballs are on top of the cabbage, otherwise it will not look anything like a lion's head.

Stirfried Kidney Flowers

Serves 4–6

230 g (8 oz) pigs' kidneys
1 tsp salt
1 tbsp cornstarch
5–6 wood ear mushrooms
60 g (2 oz) water chestnuts
40 g (1½ oz) bamboo shoots
80 g (3 oz) greens
2 scallions
1 slice fresh ginger, peeled
1 clove garlic
1 tbsp dark soy
3 tbsp stock
1 tbsp vinegar
oil for deep frying

1 Peel off the thin white skin covering the kidneys, split them in half lengthways and discard the white parts. Score the surface of the kidneys diagonally in a criss-cross pattern and then cut them into small oblong pieces. When cooked they will open up and resemble ears of corn—hence the name "flowers." Mix the kidney pieces with a little salt and ½ tbsp cornstarch.

2 Soak the wood ear mushrooms in water for about 20 minutes and slice them together with the water chestnuts and bamboo shoots. Cut and blanch the greens and finely chop the scallions, fresh ginger and garlic. Mix the remaining cornstarch with the soy sauce and stock.

3 Heat up the oil in a wok or large frying pan until it smokes; deep fry the kidney "flowers"; separate them with chopsticks or a fork, then quickly scoop them out with a slotted spoon. Now pour out the excess oil leaving about 2 tbsp in the wok; toss in the scallions, fresh ginger and garlic, add the vinegar followed by the bamboo shoots, water chestnuts, wood ear mushrooms and greens, and finally the kidneys. Pour in the sauce mixture, blend well and serve.

Stirfried Pork and Chinese White Chives

Serves 4–6

560 g (14 oz) pork fillet
2 medium dried black mushrooms
230 g (8 oz) Chinese white chives or young leeks
240 ml (8 fl oz) peanut oil
1½ tsp chopped fresh ginger
1 tsp garlic, chopped
1 tsp salt
1 tsp Chinese yellow wine or sherry

Marinade

1 tbsp light soy sauce
½ tsp sesame oil
1 egg white
1 tbsp cornstarch
2 tsp Chinese yellow wine or sherry

1 Cut the pork into 7 mm (⅛ in) thin slices, then into 5 cm (2 in) shreds. Mix the pieces of meat with the marinade and set them aside for 15 minutes.

2 Soak the black mushrooms in hot water for 30 minutes. Remove and discard the stems and cut the caps into fine shreds. Cut the chives or leeks into shreds 5 cm (2 in) long.

3 Heat the peanut oil in a pan. Add the pork, stirring to separate, reduce the heat, and leave to sit in the oil for 2 minutes. Remove, drain and set aside.

Steamed Pork Wrapped in Lotus Leaves

Serves 6–8

3–4 lotus leaves
680 g (18 oz) pork belly, thick end
2 tbsp light soy sauce
vegetable oil for deep frying
2 slices fresh ginger
2 scallions
1½ tbsp oyster sauce
1½ tsp salt
1½ tsp sugar
2 cloves garlic
3 tbsp ground rice
1½ tsp sesame oil

1 Immerse the lotus leaves in warm water for 3–4 minutes to soften. Bring a large saucepan of water to a boil, add the pork and simmer for 10 minutes. Remove and drain. Rub the pork with the soy sauce. Heat the oil in a wok or deep fryer. When hot, fry the pork for about 3 minutes. Drain. Cut the pork into 1.25 cm (½ in) slices. Finely chop the ginger and scallions. Mix together the oyster sauce, salt, sugar, ginger, garlic and scallions. Add the ground rice and sesame oil. Mix in the pork slices and make sure they are evenly coated. Pile the slices neatly into a stack, then wrap in the softened lotus leaves. Tie securely with string.

2 Place the parcel in a heatproof dish, put in a steamer and steam for 3 hours. When ready, drain away any excess water and serve straight from the lotus leaves. The pork will be tender and the ground rice will have soaked up any fattiness.

Pearl-studded Pork Balls

Serves 4–6

230 g (8 oz) glutinous rice
2 tbsp dried shrimps
450 g (1 lb) pork, ground
1 tsp salt
1½ tbsp scallion, finely chopped
1 tbsp fresh ginger, finely chopped
1 tbsp light soy sauce
1 egg
2 tbsp cornstarch

1 Soak the rice in cold water to cover for at least 8 hours. Drain well. Soak the dried shrimps in hot water to cover for 25 minutes. Drain and finely chop. Place the pork in a bowl and add the dried shrimps, salt, scallion, ginger, soy sauce, egg and 1½ tbsp of water. Combine thoroughly. Mix the soaked rice with the cornstarch. Form the pork mixture into even-sized balls and wet each ball lightly with water. Roll the balls in the rice mixture and pat on lightly to get an even covering.

2 Arrange the balls on a steaming tray in a steamer and steam vigorously for about 25 minutes. Serve on a heated dish and accompany with either soy or tomato sauce.

Sichuan Dumplings in Red Sauce

Serves 6–8

4 medium dried black mushrooms
230 g (8 oz) pork fillet
110g (4 oz) pork fat
110g (4 oz) chives or whites of scallions
2 egg whites
2 tbsp cornstarch
1 tsp salt
1 tsp sesame oil
40 wonton wrappers

Red Sauce

2 tbsp sesame oil
1 tbsp chili oil
1 tbsp garlic, chopped
1 tsp Sichuan peppercorn powder
2 tbsp sesame paste
2 tbsp dark soy sauce
1 tbsp young leek or scallion, chopped
2 tsp sugar

1   Soak the black mushrooms in hot water for 30 minutes. Remove and discard the stems. Set aside.

2   Finely dice the fillet of pork and the pork fat and chop the chives or whites of scallions into tiny pieces.

3   Place the pork, mushrooms and chives in a mixing bowl. Add 1 egg white, 1 tbsp cornstarch, 1 tsp salt and 1 tsp sesame oil and mix well.

4   Put 1 tbsp of the pork mixture in the center of a wonton wrapper. Mix the other egg white with 1 tsp cornstarch and wet two of the edges of the wrapper. Fold up the wrapper diagonally to form a triangle and press the edges to seal. Fold two opposite corners over and stick together with more of the egg white and cornstarch mixture.

5   In a large saucepan boil 5 litres (10½ pt) water and add the dumplings. When they float to the surface, add 240 ml (8 fl oz) cold water and return to a boil. Remove and drain the dumplings, arranging them in a medium-sized serving bowl (about six dumplings to each bowl). Prepare the red sauce and serve.

Sweet and Sour Spareribs

Serves 4–6
450 g (1 lb) pork spareribs
2 tbsp soy sauce
1 tbsp rice wine or dry sherry
½ tsp monosodium glutamate (optional)
2 tbsp cornstarch
2 tbsp sugar
1½ tbsp vinegar
lard for deep frying
salt and Sichuan pepper for dipping

1 Chop the spareribs into small bits using a cleaver. Mix ½ tbsp soy sauce with the rice wine or sherry and monosodium glutamate, if using. When they are all well blended together, add 1 tbsp cornstarch. Coat each piece of the spareribs with this mixture.
2 In a bowl mix the remaining soy sauce with sugar and vinegar. Warm the lard in a wok or deep fryer, put in about half of the spareribs, fry for 30 seconds, scoop them out. Wait for a while to let the lard heat up again, then fry the rest of the spareribs for 30 seconds and scoop out. Now wait for the lard to get hot before returning all the spare ribs to the wok to fry for another 50 seconds or so; scoop them out when they turn golden and place them on a serving dish.
3 Pour off the excess lard, leaving about 1 tbsp in the saucepan; add the sauce mixture. When it starts to bubble, add the remaining cornstarch mixed in a little cold water; stir to make a smooth sauce, then pour it over the spareribs.
4 Serve with salt and pepper mixed as a dip.

Pork, Carp and Salted Plum Casserole

Serves 4–6
560 g (14 oz) pork spareribs
900 g (2 lb) carp or any other freshwater fish
600 ml (1 pt) chicken stock
600 ml (1 pt) water
3–4 salted plums
6 slices fresh ginger
2 scallions

1 Chop the spareribs across the bones into bite-sized pieces and blanch them in boiling water for 2 minutes. Remove and set aside.
2 Clean the carp thoroughly, paying particular attention to the inside of the cavity. Set aside.
3 Bring the chicken stock and water to a boil in a clay pot. Add all the ingredients and when the mixture boils again, lower the heat to medium. Cook for 5 minutes. Lower the heat further and simmer gently for 15 minutes. Serve.

Spareribs in Black Bean Sauce

Serves 4–6
340 g (12 oz) pork spareribs
1 clove garlic, crushed
1 slice fresh ginger, peeled
1 small red chili
1 tsp oil

Sauce
2 tbsp crushed black bean sauce
1 tbsp soy sauce
1 tbsp rice wine or dry sherry
1 tsp cornstarch

Garnish
2 scallions, cut into short lengths
cilantro

1 Chop the spareribs into small pieces, finely chop the garlic, fresh ginger and red chili. Mix them all together with the sauce and marinate for 15 minutes.

2 Grease a heatproof plate with oil; place the spare ribs on it. Steam vigorously for 25–30 minutes. Garnish with the scallions, top with cilantro and serve.

FISH AND SHELLFISH

At first glance, shrimp may appear to be the main type of seafood used in Asian cooking. However, the range of fish and seafood available in the seas and freshwater lakes and rivers of this region is astounding, and the dishes and methods of cooking are just as varied. Fish and seafood—such as crab, clams, oysters, scallops, squid and shrimp—are steamed, roasted, grilled, fried, baked and even eaten raw.

Steamed Sea Bass with Black Mushrooms and Chinese Ham

Serves 4–6
680 g (18 oz) fillet of sea bass or any white fish
6 medium dried black mushrooms
60 g (2 oz) Chinese ham
6 scallions
6 slices fresh ginger, grated
120 ml (4 fl oz) peanut oil
1 clove garlic

Marinade
1 egg white
1 tsp cornstarch
½ tsp sesame oil
⅛ tsp pepper
1 tsp salt

Sauce
1 tbsp oyster sauce
1 tbsp light soy sauce
½ tsp sugar
1 tsp sesame oil
1 tsp Chinese yellow wine
240 ml (8 fl oz) chicken stock

1 Clean the fish and cut it into slices 5 x 3.75 cm (2 x 1½ in). Mix the marinade, add the fish pieces and set aside.

2 Soak the black mushrooms in hot water for 30 minutes. Remove and discard the stems and cut each mushroom into three or four slices. Set these aside.

3 Cut the ham into thin slices, about the same size as the fish pieces, and set aside.

4 Take four of the scallions, cutting them into 4 cm (1½ in) pieces. Use only the white part and the part immediately next to it, discarding the roots and discolored stalks.

5 Place the remaining two scallions on a large plate. Arrange the fish, ham and mushrooms in layers— one piece of fish, one piece of ham, one piece of black mushroom—on top of the scallions until all the fish, ham and mushrooms are used. Sprinkle the chopped scallions and shredded ginger on top of them.

6 Bring 1 l (2 pt) water to a boil in a wok. Put a wire rack in the wok and put the plate on top. Steam vigorously over a high heat for 5–7 minutes only.

7 Remove the plate of fish from the wok, drain and set aside.

8 Heat the oil in a saucepan. Add the garlic but remove it when it has browned and discard it. Pour the oil over the fish, draining away any excess from the plate. Add all the sauce ingredients to a saucepan, stir and bring to a boil. Pour over the fish and serve.

Steamed Whole Fish Wrapped in Lotus Leaves

Serves 4–6

1 whole fish, about 1 kg (24 oz)

1½ tbsp dark soy sauce

1 tsp salt

2 lotus leaves

3 tbsp vegetable oil

Garnish and Sauce

85–125 g (3–4 oz) tinned Chinese pickles

3 slices fresh ginger

2 scallions

2 fresh chilies

2 tbsp light soy sauce

2 tbsp rice wine or sherry

6 tbsp good stock

2 tsp sugar

1   Clean the fish and dry well. Rub inside and out with the soy sauce and salt. Shred the pickles, ginger, scallions and fresh chilies, discarding seeds. Soak the lotus leaves in warm water for 10 minutes to soften. Drain.

2   Heat the oil in a wok or frying pan. When hot, stirfry pickles, scallions, ginger and chilies over medium heat for 1 minute. Add the soy sauce, rice wine or sherry, stock and sugar, bring to a boil and stir for 30 seconds. Place the fish on the lotus leaves. Pour half the contents of the wok or frying pan over the length of the fish. Turn the fish over and pour over the remainder. Wrap the fish completely in the lotus leaves. Secure by tying with string. Place in a steamer and steam for 25 minutes.

Steamed Fish

Serves 4–6
680 g (18 oz) fish
2 tbsp cooked ham cubed
250 g (9 oz) chopped bamboo shoots
2 large Chinese dried mushrooms, soaked
15 g (½ oz) pork fat
½ tsp salt
1 tsp sugar
½ tsp monosodium glutamate (optional)
½ tbsp rice wine or sherry
2 tbsp lard
2 scallions
2 slices fresh ginger

1 Scale and gut the fish; clean and dry well. Trim off fins and tail, score the body three or four times halfway down, then place it on an oblong dish

2 Cut the ham, bamboo shoots, mushrooms and pork fat into matchstick-size shreds; arrange them in four different rows according to color in a star shape. Spread the salt, sugar, monosodium glutamate (if using), wine, lard, scallions and fresh ginger evenly on top of the fish.

3 Steam vigorously for 20 minutes; discard the scallions and fresh ginger before serving.

Cook's tip
This recipe works equally well with other whole fish, especially carp, perch or bream, but bass and trout can also be used.

Shredded Fish and Celery

Serves 4–6
230 g (8 oz) fish fillet or steak
½ tbsp rice wine or sherry
1 tsp salt
2 egg whites
½ tbsp cornstarch
240 g (8 oz) celery heart
1 tsp monosodium glutamate (optional)
2 tsp sesame oil
1½ tbsp light soy sauce
lard for deep frying
120 ml (4 fl oz) stock

Garnish
2 tbsp shredded cooked ham

1 Discard all skin and bones from the fish; cut it into matchstick-size shreds; marinate it with rice wine or sherry, salt, egg whites and cornstarch.

2 Parboil the celery heart for 1–2 minutes; cool it in cold water then cut it into small shreds. Place it on a serving plate; add ½ tsp monosodium glutamate (optional) and 1 tsp sesame oil, mix well.

3 Deep fry the fish shreds in lard over medium heat for about 4 minutes; separate them with chopsticks or a fork. When all the shreds are floating on the surface of the lard, scoop them out and drain. Gently press them with a spatula, then soak them in the stock for a while to cool. Take them out and place on top of the celery. Garnish with ham shreds.

4 Make a dressing by mixing 1 tbsp stock with the soy sauce and the remaining monosodium glutamate (optional) and sesame oil. Pour it all over the dish and serve.

Sweet and Sour Carp

Serves 4–6
680 g (18 oz) Yellow River carp
a little salt
a little all-purpose flour
oil for deep frying
40 g (1½ oz) bamboo shoots
5–6 wood ear mushrooms, soaked
4–5 water chestnuts, peeled
2–3 scallions
2 slices fresh ginger, peeled
1 clove garlic, finely chopped
1 carrot, finely chopped

Sauce
3 tbsp wine vinegar
3 tbsp sugar
2 tbsp soy sauce
2 tbsp rice wine or sherry
2 tsp cornstarch
120 ml (4 fl oz) clear stock

1 Scale and gut the carp and clean thoroughly. Score the fish on both sides diagonally in a criss-cross pattern down to the bone. Lift the fish up by the ends so the cuts open up, spread a little salt into them followed by a little flour, then coat the whole fish from head to tail with flour.

2 Cut the wood ear mushrooms into thin slices together with the bamboo shoots and water chestnuts. Shred the scallions and fresh ginger into the size of matches, and finely chop the garlic.

3 Heat the oil in a wok until it smokes. Holding the fish by the tail, gently lower it into the hot oil, bending the body so that the cuts open up; use a spatula beneath the body to prevent it from sticking to the wok. After 2 minutes turn the fish on its side with its stomach facing up, still holding the tail to make sure the body is kept curved. Cook for 2 more minutes, then turn the fish over so that its stomach is now facing down; after 2 minutes cook the fish on its flat side again, tilting the wok so that the head is in the oil. When the fish has been cooked for 8 minutes in all, take it out (carefully!) and place it on a long dish.

4 Pour off the excess oil in the wok. Fry the scallions, fresh ginger and garlic; add the vinegar followed by the rest of the sauce ingredients, stir and bring to a boil; pour it all over the fish and serve. Sprinkle carrot over to serve.

Stir-fried Squid and Broccoli

Serves 4–6
450 g (1 lb) squid
2 slices fresh ginger, peeled
2 tsp salt
1 tbsp rice wine or sherry
1 tbsp cornstarch
500 ml (17 fl oz) broccoli florets
4 tbsp oil
1 tsp sesame oil
2 scallions
1 tsp sugar

1 Clean the squid; discard the head and transparent backbone as well as the ink sac; make a criss-cross pattern on the outside, then cut into pieces about the size of a matchbox. Mix with 1 slice finely chopped fresh ginger, 1 tsp salt, rice wine or sherry and cornstarch.

2 Cut the broccoli into small florets, scallions into 2.5 cm (1 in) lengths, and grate the remaining slice of fresh ginger.

3 Heat up 2 tbsp oil, toss in the scallions and fresh ginger, followed by the broccoli; add salt and sugar, stir for 2 minutes; remove and put aside.

Steamed Sea Bass

Serves 4–6
900 g (2 lb) sea bass
20 g (¾ oz) bamboo shoots
2–3 Chinese dried mushrooms, soaked
2 slices fresh ginger, peeled
2 scallions
1 leek
3 tbsp soy sauce
1 tbsp oil
½ tbsp sugar
1 tbsp rice wine or sherry
2 tbsp stock
1 tsp salt
sesame oil to serve

1 Scale and gut the fish, clean thoroughly, then plunge it into a pot of boiling water; take it out as soon as the water starts to boil again. Place it on a long dish.

2 Shred the bamboo shoots, mushrooms, fresh ginger, scallions and leek; place them on top of the fish, then pour the soy sauce, oil, sugar, rice wine or sherry, stock and salt over it. Steam vigorously for 20 minutes.

3 Heat up the remaining oil, stirfry the squid for about 1 minute; add the broccoli; blend well. Add a drizzle of sesame oil and serve.

Sole in Sweet and Sour Sauce

Serves 4–6
230 g (8 oz) sole fillet (or alternatively plaice fillet)
2 tbsp cornstarch
600 ml (1 pt) oil for deep frying

Sauce
1 tbsp lard
1 tbsp sugar
1 tbsp soy sauce
1 tbsp vinegar
1 tbsp rice wine or sherry
1 tbsp cornstarch
½ tsp monosodium glutamate (optional)
1 slice fresh ginger, finely chopped
1 scallion, finely chopped

1 Cut the fish into small, thin slices and coat them with cornstarch.
2 Heat the oil in a wok or deep fryer over a high heat until smoking. Then reduce the heat and use a pair of chopsticks to put the fish slices into the oil and deep fry them for about 2 minutes or until golden. Remove and drain.
3 Heat up the lard in a wok or frying pan; meanwhile, mix the sugar, soy sauce, vinegar, wine or sherry, cornstarch and monosodium glutamate (if using) in a bowl. Toss the finely chopped fresh ginger and scallion into the hot lard, then pour in the sauce mixture and stir until thickened; now add the fish slices; blend well so that each piece is coated with the sauce, then serve.

Fried Bass in Sweet and Sour Sauce

Serves 4–6
680–900 g (1½–2 lb) sea bass
1 tsp salt
2 tbsp flour
oil for deep frying

Sauce
2 tbsp sugar
2 tbsp vinegar
1 tbsp soy sauce
½ tbsp cornstarch
2 tbsp stock or water

Garnish
2 scallions
2 slices fresh ginger, peeled
1 small red pepper
fresh cilantro

1 Clean and de-scale the fish, slash both sides diagonally at intervals. Rub salt both inside and out, then coat with flour.
2 Thinly shred the scallions, fresh ginger and red pepper.
3 Deep fry the fish in hot oil until golden; place it on a long dish.
4 Pour off the excess oil from the wok, put in the sauce mixture and stir until smooth, then pour it over the fish. Garnish with shredded scallions, fresh ginger, red pepper and fresh cilantro.

Squid with Shrimp Balls in Black Bean Sauce

Serves 4–6

450 g (1 lb) squid
500 g (16 oz) green peppers
1 slice fresh ginger, peeled
1 scallion
2 green chilies
oil for deep frying
1 tsp salt
1 tsp sugar
1 tbsp crushed black bean sauce
1 tbsp rice wine or sherry
1 tbsp soy sauce
20 deep-fried shrimp balls

1 Discard the soft bone, head and ink sac of the squid; peel off the skin and make a criss-cross pattern on the outside, then cut into slices not much bigger than a matchbox.

2 Cut the green peppers into slices roughly the same size as the squid, finely chop the fresh ginger, scallion and green chili.

3 Deep fry the squid for 1 minute, remove and drain. Pour off the excess oil, leaving about 2 tbsp in the wok. Toss in the fresh ginger, scallion and chilies followed by green peppers; add salt and sugar; stir for a short while then add the squid together with the crushed black bean sauce, rice wine or sherry and soy sauce. Cook for about 1½ minutes and blend everything well. Serve with deep-fried shrimp balls decorating the edge of the plate.

Chrysanthemum Fish Pot

Serves 4–6

110 g (4 oz) fish maw
2 chicken gizzards
10 g (4 oz) sea cucumber
230 g (8 oz) tripe
5450 g (1 lb) Chinese cabbage
1110 g (4 oz) green peppers
230 g (8 oz) spinach leaves
60 g (2 oz) fresh cilantro
2 slices fresh ginger, peeled
2–6 scallions
2 tsp salt
1 tsp freshly ground Sichuan pepper
2 litres (4 pt) stock
110 g (4 oz) chicken breast meat, de-boned and skinned
1 large dried chrysanthemum (white or yellow)

1 Cut the fish maw, chicken gizzard, sea cucumber and tripe into slices. Wash the cabbage, green peppers, spinach and cilantro; cut them into small pieces.

2 Finely chop the fresh ginger and scallions; place them with salt and pepper in a small bowl.

3 Bring the stock to a rolling boil in the fire-pot; arrange the meat and vegetables in the moat. They will only need to be cooked for about 5 minutes. Everybody just helps themselves from the pot with chopsticks. Use the chrysanthemum as a decoration.

Fish in Hot Sauce

Serves 4–6
680 g (18 oz) freshwater fish
oil for deep frying
2 tbsp chili paste
1 tbsp tomato paste
1 tbsp soy sauce
2 tbsp rice wine or sherry
½ tbsp sugar
240 ml (8 fl oz) stock
2 slices fresh ginger, peeled and finely chopped
1 clove garlic, finely chopped
1 tbsp vinegar
2 scallions, finely chopped
1 tbsp cornstarch

1 Scale and gut the fish, clean well. Slash each side diagonally four or five times as deep as the bone.
2 Heat the oil, deep fry the fish until golden, turning it over once or twice; remove and drain.
3 Pour off the excess oil, leaving about 1 tbsp in the wok; put in the chili paste, tomato paste, soy sauce, rice wine or sherry, sugar, stock, ginger and garlic. Bring to a boil, put the fish back; reduce heat and cook gently for a few minutes, turning it over two or three times. Place the fish on a serving dish. Increase the heat, add vinegar and scallions to the sauce, thicken it with the cornstarch then pour it over the fish and serve.

Braised Whole Fish in Hot Vinegar Sauce

Serves 4–6
2 slices fresh ginger
680–900 g (1½–2 lb) whole fish
1 tsp salt
pepper to taste
2 tsp fresh ginger, chopped
4 tbsp vegetable oil

Sauce
3 slices fresh ginger, peeled
80 ml (2⅔ fl oz) tinned bamboo shoots, drained
½ red pepper
1 small carrot
1 green chili
2 dried chilies
2 scallions
2 tbsp lard
2 tbsp light soy sauce
3 tbsp good stock
6 tbsp vinegar
½ tbsp cornstarch blended with 2 tbsp water

1 Finely chop the 2 slices of ginger. Clean the fish and dry well. Rub evenly inside and out with salt, pepper, chopped ginger and 1 tbsp of the oil. Leave to season for 30 minutes. Shred the 3 slices of ginger, bamboo shoots, red pepper, carrot, chilies (discarding the seeds) and scallions.
2 Heat the remaining oil in a wok or frying pan. When hot, fry the fish for 2½ minutes on each side. Remove and drain. Add the shredded ginger, bamboo shoots, red pepper, carrot, chilies and scallions to the remaining oil and stirfry over medium heat for 1 minute. Add the lard, soy sauce, stock and half the vinegar and cook for another minute. Lay the fish back in the wok or saucepan and cook gently for 2 minutes on both sides, basting. Transfer the fish to a serving dish. Stir the remaining vinegar into the wok, then add the blended cornstarch, stirring over high heat until the sauce thickens.
3 Pour the sauce from the wok over the length of the fish and garnish with the shredded vegetables.

Tofu Fish in Chili Sauce

Serves 4–6

450 g (1 lb) mullet or mackerel
1 clove garlic
2 slices fresh ginger, peeled
2 scallions, white parts only
2 tofu cakes
360 ml (12 fl oz) stock
1 tsp salt
4 tbsp oil
2 tbsp chili paste
1 tbsp soy sauce
2 tbsp rice wine or sherry
1 tbsp cornstarch

1 Cut the heads off the fish and remove the backbones; crush the garlic, cut it and the fresh ginger into small pieces; cut the scallion whites into short lengths.

2 Cut each tofu into about 10 pieces. Blanch them in boiling water; remove and soak them in stock with salt.

3 Heat the oil until hot; fry the fish until both sides are golden; put them aside; tilt the wok, and put in the chili paste. When it starts to bubble, return the wok to its original position, push the fish back, add soy sauce, rice wine or sherry, scallions, fresh ginger, garlic and a little stock—about 120 ml (4 fl oz). At the same time add the tofu taken from the stock and cook with the fish for about 10 minutes.

4 Now pick out the fish with chopsticks and place them on a serving dish, then quickly mix the cornstarch with a little cold water. Add to the wok to make a smooth sauce with the tofu; pour it all over the fish and serve.

Fish and Tofu Casserole

Serves 2–4

110 g (4 oz) fish steak
80 ml (2⅔ fl oz) chopped cooked ham
1 slice fresh ginger, peeled
1 scallion
600 ml (1¼ pt) stock
1 tsp salt
freshly ground Sichuan pepper
2 tofu cakes
1 tbsp cornstarch
2 egg whites
1 tsp sesame oil
2 tbsp oil
fresh cilantro

1 Cut the fish into thin strips. Coarsely chop the tofu and finely chop the ham. Shred the fresh ginger and scallion.

2 Heat the oil; toss in the fresh ginger followed by the fish; stir gently for a while; add stock, salt, Sichuan pepper and tofu; bring it to a boil. Thicken with cornstarch mixed with a little water, then add egg whites, sesame oil and the scallion; blend well. Transfer to a dish or serve in a casserole dish garnished with chopped ham and fresh cilantro.

Sweet-sour Crispy Fish

Serves 2–3
680 g (18 oz) carp (or freshwater fish)
2 tbsp rice wine or sherry
4 tbsp soy sauce
6 tbsp cornstarch
1 clove garlic
2 scallions
2 slices fresh ginger
2 dried red chilies, soaked
20 g (1½ oz) bamboo shoots
2–3 dried Chinese mushrooms, soaked
oil for deep frying
1½ tbsp sugar
1½ tbsp vinegar
120 ml (4 fl oz) stock

1 Clean the fish; make 6 or 7 diagonal cuts as deep as the bone on each side of the fish. Marinate in rice wine or sherry and 2 tbsp of soy sauce for 15 minutes; remove and wipe dry. Make a paste with 4½ tbsp cornstarch and water and coat the entire fish evenly.

2 Finely chop the garlic, 1 scallion and 1 slice ginger. Cut the other scallion and fresh ginger into thin shreds. Cut the soaked red chilies (discarding the seeds), bamboo shoots and mushrooms into thin shreds.

3 Heat the oil to boiling point, pick up the fish by the tail, lower it head-first into the oil, turn it around and deep fry for about 7 minutes or until golden; remove and drain.

4 Pour off the excess oil leaving about 2 tbsp in the wok; add finely chopped scallion, fresh ginger, garlic and red chili, bamboo shoots and mushrooms followed by the remaining soy sauce, sugar, vinegar and stock. Stir a few times, then add the remaining cornstarch mixed with a little water; blend well to make a slightly thick smooth sauce.

5 Place a cloth over the fish, press gently with your hand to soften the body, then put it on a serving dish and pour the sauce over it; garnish with scallion and fresh ginger shreds.

Sizzling Eel

Serves 4–6
900 g (2 lb) yellow eel
2.4 l (5 pt) boiling water
4 tbsp peanut oil
2 tsp fresh ginger, chopped
½ tsp pepper
2 tsp Chinese yellow wine
1 tbsp sugar
2 tbsp dark soy sauce
8 tbsp chicken stock
1½ tbsp cornstarch dissolved in 1½ tbsp water
2 tsp scallions, chopped
2 tbsp sesame oil
2 tsp ham, ground
1½ tsp fresh cilantro, chopped

1 Place the eels in a basin. Pour over them a boiling water (to which has been added 2 tbsp salt) and let them stand for 3 minutes. Take the eels out of the water and rinse them in cold water from the faucet.

2 Separate the meat from the bone with the handle of a teaspoon, then cut the eel meat into 0.5 x 5 cm (¼ x 2 in) strips. Set aside. Heat the oil until very hot. Add the eel, stirring, and add the chopped ginger, pepper, yellow wine, sugar, soy sauce and chicken stock. Cook for 5 minutes. Stir in the cornstarch and transfer to a plate. Make a small well in the center of the eels and put into it the chopped scallions.

3 Heat 2 tbsp sesame oil until very hot and pour it into the "well". Add the ham, garnish with cilantro and serve.

Steamed Eel

Serves 4–6
900 g (2 lb) white eel
2 tbsp salt
6 slices fresh ginger
2 scallions
8 tbsp peanut oil
1 tsp Chinese yellow wine
240 ml (8 fl oz) chicken stock
1 tsp sugar
½ tsp pepper
1 tbsp cornstarch

1 Put the eel in a basin and pour over it 1.2 litres (2¼ pt) boiling water with salt added. Wash the fish thoroughly. Slit the eel open, remove the intestines and clean the insides carefully. Pat it dry with paper towels.

2 Make deep cuts (about three-quarters of the way through the flesh) at 2½ cm (1 in) intervals along the eel and place it on a plate, bending it into a ring form. Arrange the ginger and scallions on top.

3 Steam the eel over medium heat for 20 minutes. Remove the ginger and scallions, discard them and drain the liquid from the plate. Heat the oil and pour it over the eel, again draining any excess from the plate.

4 Add the remaining ingredients to the saucepan, stir and bring to a boil. Pour the sauce over the eel and serve.

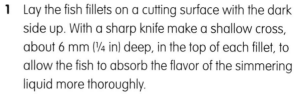

Sole Simmered in Sake

Serves 4

4 x 85 g (3 oz) sole fillet

1 tsp salt

1 tbsp fresh ginger, grated

140 ml (6 fl oz) dashi

4 tbsp sake

4 tbsp dark soy sauce

4 tbsp rice wine or sherry

10 g (⅓ oz) dried wakame seaweed,
 reconstituted

1 Lay the fish fillets on a cutting surface with the dark side up. With a sharp knife make a shallow cross, about 6 mm (¼ in) deep, in the top of each fillet, to allow the fish to absorb the flavor of the simmering liquid more thoroughly.

2 Arrange the fillets on a strainer and sprinkle with a little salt; set aside to drain for at least 1 hour. Rinse in cold water and then pat dry. Peel the ginger and slice thinly.

3 Combine the dashi, sake, soy sauce, rice wine and salt in a large saucepan and bring to a boil. Arrange the fish in an individual layer in the simmering stock, with the dark side on top.

4 Add the ginger. Return to a boil, carefully skim the surface, cover and cook over medium heat, occasionally ladling the simmering stock over the fish pieces, until the stock is reduced by half.

5 Cut the reconstituted wakame into 2.5 cm (1 in) pieces and add to the simmering stock. Continue to simmer for a few more minutes until the stock is thick and much reduced. Turn off the heat and leave the fish for a few minutes in the hot stock before serving.

6 To serve, remove the fish from the saucepan using a fish slice. Arrange in individual bowls and distribute the wakame and ginger evenly. Pour over a little of the simmering stock and serve.

Fukien Clam Soup

Serves 4–5

1.5 kg (3 lb) clams
2 tbsp salt
1½ tbsp dried shrimp
2 slices fresh ginger
3 scallions
2 cloves garlic
2 tsp salt
pepper to taste
1½ chicken stock cubes
1 l (2 pt) light soy sauce
1 tbsp vinegar
½ tsp sesame oil

1 Wash and clean the clams well with a stiff brush under running water. Bring 1.2 litres (2½ pt) water to a boil in a saucepan and add the salt. Simmer the clams for 2 minutes then leave to stand in the water, off the heat, for one more minute. Drain. Discard any unopened clams. Soak the shrimp in hot water for 5 minutes, then drain. Finely shred the ginger and scallions. Crush the garlic.

2 Place the poached clams in a saucepan. Add the shrimp, ginger, garlic, salt, pepper and crumbled stock cube. Bring to a boil. Reduce the heat and simmer for 10 minutes. Add the scallions, soy sauce and vinegar, and continue to simmer for another 5 minutes.

3 Place the clams and soup in a large heated serving bowl and sprinkle over the sesame oil. Serve in single bowls and eat like *mussels marinière*, or the dish can be eaten from a large central bowl.

Fu Yung Crabmeat

Serves 4
3 tbsp lard
1 slice fresh ginger, peeled and finely chopped
2 scallions, finely chopped
280 g (10 oz) crabmeat
2 tbsp rice wine or sherry
6 egg whites
2 large crab shells (or 4 small ones)
2 cloves garlic, finely chopped
1 tbsp soy sauce
1 tbsp wine vinegar
1 tbsp sugar
3 tbsp stock
1 tsp cornstarch

1 Warm up about 2 tbsp lard; fry about half of the finely chopped fresh ginger and scallions followed by the crabmeat. Add rice wine or sherry, continue stirring until all the liquid has evaporated, then put the crabmeat into the empty shells.
2 Beat the egg whites with salt and a little water until foamy; pour on top of the crabmeat and steam the stuffed shells vigorously for 6 minutes. By then the egg whites will have become solid. Remove and place them on a long serving dish.
3 Heat the last tbsp lard, add the garlic and the remaining scallion and fresh ginger, followed by soy sauce, vinegar, sugar and stock. When it starts to bubble, add the cornstarch mixed with a little cold water. When it is smooth and thickened pour it over the crabmeat and serve.

Aromatic Chiu Chow Rich Fish Soup

Serves 4–6
140 g (5 oz) fillet of sea bream or other white fish
110 g (4 oz) squid
1 tsp sesame oil
1 tsp salt
1 fillet dried sole
2–3 tbsp peanut oil
2 medium dried black mushrooms
1 stick celery
600 ml (1 pt) chicken stock
150 g (5 oz) plain cooked rice

1 Cut the fillet of fish into thick slices and cut the squid into bite-sized pieces. Mix the fish and squid with 1 tsp sesame oil and 1 tsp salt.
2 Break or chop the dried sole into tiny pieces and fry with 2–3 tbsp oil over low heat until crisp. Drain and set aside.
3 Soak the black mushrooms in hot water for 30 minutes. Remove and discard the stems and cut the caps into fine shreds. Chop the celery coarsely. Bring the chicken stock to a boil and add the celery, black mushrooms and rice. When the soup boils again, add the sliced fish and squid and when it boils again, sprinkle with the chopped dried fish.

Crab Balls

Serves 6–8
230 g (8 oz) crabmeat
46 g (1½ oz) pork fat
60 g (2 oz) water chestnuts, peeled
2 eggs
2 tbsp rice wine or sherry
1 tsp monosodium glutamate (optional)
1 tsp salt
2 tbsp cornstarch
1 slice fresh ginger, finely chopped
1 scallion, finely chopped
450 g (1 lb) lard for deep frying
120 ml (4 fl oz) chicken stock
30 g (1 oz) cooked ham, finely chopped

1   Finely chop the crabmeat, pork fat and water chestnuts and add 2 eggs, 1 tbsp rice wine or sherry, ½ tsp monosodium glutamate (if using), ½ tsp salt, and 1 tbsp cornstarch together with the ginger and scallions. Blend well, then make into small balls about the size of walnuts.

2   Heat the lard over high heat for 3–4 minutes, then reduce the heat to moderate and deep fry the crab balls for about 5 minutes until pale golden. Scoop them out with a slotted spoon and serve them hot or cold. Alternatively, place them in a bowl with a little chicken stock—not quite enough to cover them—then place the bowl in a steamer and steam for 15 minutes.

3   Now mix the remaining wine or sherry, monosodium glutamate (if using), salt and cornstarch with the chicken stock and cook over a moderate heat to make a white sauce, then pour it over the crab balls. Garnish with finely chopped ham and serve.

Deep-fried Crab Balls

Serves 4
2 pieces dried tofu sheet
230 g (8 oz) shrimp, shelled and deveined
70 g (2½ oz) pork fat
85 g (3 oz) water chestnuts
1 egg white
2 tbsp cornstarch
1 tbsp chopped leek, white part only
1 tbsp chopped scallion
1 tsp salt
½ tsp pepper
110 g (4 oz) crabmeat
700 ml (1½ pt) peanut oil

1   Soak the dried tofu sheets in water until softened. Remove and pat dry. Set aside. Grind or finely chop the shrimp and dice the pork fat and water chestnuts into small pieces.

2   Place the shrimp, egg white and cornstarch in a mixing bowl and stir in one direction until the mixture becomes sticky and firm. Add the pork and continue stirring until the mixture is thickened.

3   Add the water chestnuts, stirring well, and the leek, scallion, salt and pepper and the crabmeat, mixing each ingredient in thoroughly.

4   Place a tofu sheet on a board. Put the shrimp and crabmeat mixture down the center about 2.5 cm (1 in) diameter. Roll the tofu sheet firmly around the mixture, trimming off any excess at the ends.

5   Place the "sausage" on a heatproof platter, and steam it over high heat for 7 minutes. Remove, set aside and when it has cooled, cut it into 4 cm (1½ in) slices.

6   Heat the oil in a saucepan. When it is hot, add the crabmeat slices. Reduce the heat to low and fry until the tofu wrapper is nicely golden in color. Serve with Chiu Chow tangerine jam.

Crab Casserole

Serves 4-6
2 crabs—approximately 580 g (14 oz) each
1 tbsp cornstarch
700 ml (1½ pt) peanut oil
2 tsp chopped garlic
3–4 slices fresh ginger
2 scallions

Seasonings
8 tbsp good stock
1 tbsp oyster sauce
1 tsp oil
few drops sesame oil
1 tsp sugar
1 tsp rice wine

1 Clean the crabs and crush the pincers. Chop each crab into six pieces. Dry and dust with cornstarch.
2 Heat the peanut oil and fry the crabs for 1 minute. Remove the crab from the saucepan and drain the oil.
3 Heat the large saucepan or wok. Add the garlic, ginger and scallions and sauté for 15 seconds to release their aromatic flavors. Mix and turn them quickly with the crab before transferring the mixture to a casserole dish.
4 Add the seasonings. Cover the pot and cook for 2 minutes over high heat, turning the contents from time to time.
5 Serve in the casserole dish.

Steamed Lobster

Serves 2–4
680–900 g (1½–2 lb) lobster

Sauce
1 tbsp oil
2 scallions, finely chopped
2 slices fresh ginger, finely chopped
1 tsp salt
1 tsp sugar
4 tbsp stock
freshly ground Sichuan pepper
½ tbsp cornstarch
1 tsp sesame oil

1 Steam the lobster for 20 minutes. Leave to cool, then split in half lengthways, and cut each half into four pieces.
2 Crack the shells of the claws so that the flesh can be taken out easily.
3 Make the sauce by heating the oil in a wok or saucepan; toss in the scallions and fresh ginger; add salt, sugar, stock and ground pepper. Thicken with the cornstarch mixed with a little water. Finally add the sesame oil; pour it all over the lobster and serve.

Stuffed Crab Shell

Serves 4
1 tsp sugar
2 scallions, sliced finely
2 red chilies, finely chopped
30 g (1 oz) cilantro leaves
50 g (1¼ oz) crabmeat
80 g (2 oz) shrimp, shelled and deveined
160 g (5 oz) pork, mince
1 tsp ground white pepper
¼ tsp salt
¼ tsp light soy sauce
3 eggs
4 blue crab shells, cleaned well
1.2 litres (4 fl oz) oil for deep frying

1 Mix together sugar, scallion, chili, cilantro leaves, crabmeat, shrimp (ground or chopped), pork, pepper, salt and soy sauce.
2 Take crab shells and stuff with the pork mixture.
3 Mix the eggs well in bowl. Heat the oil in a pot to approx. 180°C/350°F/Gas Mark 4. Dip the stuffed crabs in the eggs and then fry in the oil until thoroughly cooked. Remove and drain well. Place on plates and sprinkle with more cilantro and chili. Serve as hors d"oeuvres or with rice and Chinese plum sauce (available at most supermarkets).

Deep-fried Oysters

Serves 4–6
20–25 medium oysters
1 tsp salt
pepper to taste
2 tsp finely chopped fresh ginger
vegetable oil for deep frying
1½ tbsp scallions, finely chopped

Batter
1 egg
5 tbsp all-purpose flour
1 tbsp cornstarch
5 tbsp water
½ tsp baking powder

1 Shell and drain the oysters. Sprinkle with salt, pepper and ginger. Combine the ingredients for the batter until smooth.
2 Heat the oil in a wok or deep fryer. When very hot, dip the oysters individually into the batter. Fry in batches for 3 minutes until golden brown. Drain. Transfer to a heated serving dish and sprinkle with scallion.

Oyster Omelet

Serves 2
4 medium oysters
1 tbsp cornstarch
4 eggs
2 scallions
1 stem fresh cilantro
½ tsp sesame oil
1 tsp pepper
1 tsp salt
2 tbsp peanut oil

1 Clean the oysters, cut them into small pieces (5 mm (¼ in)) and mix them with the cornstarch. Set aside.
2 Beat the eggs together lightly until well mixed. Chop the scallions and cilantro into fine shavings and add to the egg.
3 Blanch the diced oysters in boiling water for 30 seconds. Drain and add the sesame oil, pepper and salt. Mix well.
4 Heat a saucepan over medium heat and add 2 tbsp peanut oil. Pour half of the egg mixture into the saucepan and half of the diced oysters. When the edge of the omelet browns slightly, turn it over cooking. Repeat with the rest of the egg and diced oysters. Serve in a warmed dish.

Rice in Lotus Leaves

Serves 4
500 g (1 lb) long-grain rice
150 g (5 oz) dried scallops or dried shrimp
2½ l (5 pt) water
150 g (5 oz) roast duck
110 g (4 oz) fresh shrimp
100 g (3½ oz) crabmeat
2 tbsp chopped ham
1 tsp sesame oil
¼ tsp pepper
1 tbsp soy sauce
1 tsp salt
1 large dried lotus leaf

1 Wash and drain the rice. Put the scallops into the water and boil them over low heat until only about half of the water is left.
2 Put the rice in a large bowl or basin together with the scallop soup and steam the mixture for 15–20 minutes.
3 Mix the steamed rice and scallops with all the other ingredients and wrap the rice mixture in a large lotus leaf, which has been cleaned by rinsing under boiling water and steamed for 30 minutes. Secure the lotus package with string and place it in a steamer to steam for another 10 minutes.
4 Serve by bringing the "package" to the table, to be unwrapped.

Sweet and Sour Shrimp

Serves 4–6
450 g (1 lb) large uncooked shrimp, shelled and deveined
1 egg white
1½ tbsp cornstarch
1 scallion, finely chopped
2 slices fresh ginger, peeled
oil for deep frying
2 tbsp sugar
2 tbsp chicken stock

1 Cut each shrimp in half lengthways. Make a criss-cross pattern on each half and marinate them with the egg white and cornstarch.

2 Finely chop the scallion and fresh ginger. Heat up about 1 litre (2 pt) oil in a wok and, before the oil gets too hot, add the shrimp, one by one. Fry until golden, take them out and drain.

3 Leave about 1 tbsp oil on the wok; stirfry the scallion and fresh ginger until softened. then add in the shrimp; stir and add sugar and continue stirring until all the sugar has dissolved. Add the remaining cornstarch mixed with the chicken stock and blend well, then serve.

Quick-fried Shrimp

Serves 4–6
240 g (8 oz) large shrimp, uncooked
500 g (15 oz) lard for deep frying
1½ tbsp soy sauce
1 tbsp rice wine or sherry
½ tbsp sugar
1 scallion, finely chopped
1 stick fresh ginger, peeled and finely chopped
½ tbsp vinegar

1 Trim the shrimp, but keep the shells on. Dry well.
2 Heat the lard in a wok and when it is bubbling deep fry the shrimp twice (3–4 seconds only each time); scoop out and drain.
3 Pour out all the lard, then return the shrimp to the same wok. Add soy sauce, rice wine, sugar, scallions and fresh ginger; stir a few times; add vinegar and serve.

"Dragon-Well" Shrimp

Serves 4–6
450 g (1 lb) large freshwater shrimp
1 tsp salt
¼ tsp monosodium glutamate (optional)
1 egg white
1 tbsp cornstarch
lard for deep frying
1 tbsp rice wine or sherry

1 Shell the shrimp, put them in cold water and stir with chopsticks for 2–3 minutes. Change the water two or three times, then drain. Mix them with the salt, monosodium glutamate (if using), egg white and the cornstarch; marinate for 3 hours.
2 Heat the lard and deep fry the shrimp, separate them with chopsticks after 15 seconds or so, scoop them out and drain. Pour off the excess lard, return the shrimp to the wok, add the wine, and stir a few times. It is then ready to serve.

Salt and Pepper Shrimp

Serves 4-6

450 g (1 lb) large shrimp
8 tbsp vegetable oil
2 cloves garlic
2 dried red chilies
2 scallions
1½ tsp Sichuan peppercorns
1½ tsp salt

1 Wash and shell the shrimp. Sprinkle on 1½ tsp of the oil. Cut the scallions into 2.5 cm (1 in) sections. Thinly slice the garlic. Shred the chilies. Lightly pound the peppercorns and mix with the salt.

2 Heat the remaining oil in a wok or frying pan. When hot, stirfry the shrimp over a high heat for 1 minute. Remove the shrimp and pour away the oil to use for other purposes, except for 1 tbsp. Reheat the oil in the wok or frying pan. When hot, quickly stirfry the chili, garlic and scallions. Spread out the scallions and chili and return the shrimp. Sprinkle on the salt and pepper mixture and stirfry for another 45 seconds.

Three Delicacies Stuffed with Shrimp

Serves 4
1 eggplant
4 green peppers
4 tomatoes
110 g (4 oz) pork fat
350 g (12 oz) fresh shelled shrimp
few drops sesame oil
2 tbsp cornstarch
2 tbsp peanut oil

Seasonings
1 egg white
1 tsp cornstarch
½ tsp salt
¼ tsp peppers

Sauce
1 tbsp tomato juice
2 tsp ketchup
2 tsp soy sauce
5 tbsp chicken stock
1 tsp sugar

1. Cut the eggplant into slices 1.75 cm (½ in) thick and cut a slit in each piece.
2. Cut the green peppers in half and remove the seeds, and cut the tomatoes in half and remove the pulp.
3. Dice the pork fat finely. Chop and mash the shrimp into a paste, continuing to stir and beat the paste until it becomes sticky.
4. Add the diced pork fat and continue to stir, and then mix the seasonings with the shrimp paste. Refrigerate for 2 hours. Coat the inside of the eggplant, green peppers and tomatoes with cornstarch and stuff them with the shrimp mixture. Heat a frying pan over a high heat. Add 2 tbsp oil and fry the vegetables, open side down, over a medium heat for 1½ minutes.
5. Mix and blend the sauce ingredients in a bowl and pour the mixture evenly over the stuffed vegetables. Cover the frying pan and cook for 2 more minutes, then serve piping hot.

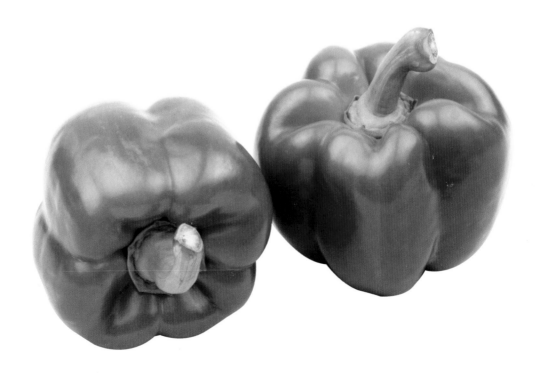

Braised Shrimp

Serves 4–6

240 g (8 oz) shrimp, unshelled
oil for deep frying
1 tbsp rice wine or sherry
4 tbsp stock
4 dried red chilies, soaked and finely chopped
1 tbsp chili paste
½ tbsp *Kaoliang* spirit
1 slice fresh ginger, peeled and finely chopped
1 scallion, finely chopped
1 tsp salt
½ tsp Sichuan pepper
2 tbsp tomato paste
1 tbsp cornstarch
½ tsp sesame oil

1 Clean the shrimp, cut them into two or three pieces but keep the shells on.
2 Heat up the oil and deep fry the shrimp until they turn bright pink. Scoop them out and pour off the excess oil. Put the shrimp back in the frying pan, together with the rice wine or sherry and a little stock; cook for about 1 minute; remove.
3 Heat about 1 tbsp oil in the wok; add the red chilies, chili paste, *Kaoliang* spirit, fresh ginger, scallion, salt and pepper, the remaining stock and the shrimp. Reduce heat and braise for 2 minutes, then add the tomato paste and the cornstarch mixed with a little water. Blend well; add sesame oil and serve.

Wine-marinated Shrimp

Serves 4–6
240 g (8 oz) large fresh shrimp
3 tbsp rice wine or sherry
2 scallions, white parts only
40 g (1½ oz) celery
40 g (1½ oz) carrots
1 tbsp peas

Sauce
2 tbsp soy sauce
1 tsp sesame oil

1 Wash the shrimp well, and place in a dish. Pour the wine or sherry over them, add the scallion whites cut to 2.5 cm (1 in) lengths and then cover and marinate for 5 minutes.
2 Slice the celery and carrot; parboil with the peas for 5 minutes. Drain and add to the shrimp. Mix together both the sauce ingredients and then pour it over the shrimp and serve.

Squid Stuffed with Shrimp

Serves 4–6
110 g (4 oz) dried squid
110 g (4 oz) pork fat
400 g (14 oz) shrimp, shelled and deveined
2 tbsp cornstarch
½ tsp pepper
¼ tsp salt
1 egg white

1 Soak the dried squid in hot water for 1 hour before cutting it into pieces 3.5 x 6 cm (1½ x 2½ in).
2 Cut the pork fat into 3mm (⅛ in) cubes and blanch in boiling water for 2 minutes. Remove and drain.
3 Pound the shrimp with the flat side of a cleaver and place them in a mixing bowl. Add 1 tbsp cornstarch, the salt and pepper and the egg white to the shrimp and, using a fork, stir in one direction only until the mixture becomes sticky. Add the pork fat and stir until sticky again. Set aside.
4 Take a piece of squid and dust one side with some of the remaining cornstarch. Place 1 tbsp of the shrimp and pork fat mixture on the flavored side of the squid and press gently. Continue until all the squid pieces and shrimp mixture are used.
5 Arrange the stuffed squid on a plate and steam for 10 minutes over high heat.

Fried Squid with Peppers

Serves 4–6
340 g (12 oz) squid
1 red pepper
2 slices fresh ginger, peeled
oil for deep frying
1 tsp salt
1 tbsp rice wine or sherry
1 tbsp soy sauce
½ tsp freshly ground black pepper
1 tsp vinegar
1 tsp sesame oil
fresh cilantro

1   Discard the head, transparent backbone and ink
    sac of the squid. Peel off the thin skin and score
    a criss-cross pattern on the outside, then cut into
    small pieces the size of a matchbox.
2   Thinly shred the red pepper and fresh ginger.
3   Deep fry the squid in oil over moderate heat for
    30 seconds; scoop out and drain. Pour off the
    excess oil, leaving about 1 tbsp in the wok; toss in
    the fresh ginger and red pepper followed by the
    squid; add salt, rice wine or sherry, soy sauce,
    black pepper and vinegar. Stirfry for about
    1 minute, add sesame oil and serve. Garnish
    with fresh cilantro.

VEGETABLES

In many Asian dishes vegetables are the main ingredient. For some Asian people, religion dictates that they should follow a vegetarian diet, but in poorer parts of the continent, vegetables have often been the only food that people could afford to eat. Over the centuries, therefore, elaborate recipes that use complex and exciting flavors have been developed to make the most of the abundance of fresh vegetables on offer.

Eggplant with Sichuan "Fish Sauce"

Serves 4–6
4–5 dried red chilies
450 g (1 lb) eggplant
oil for deep frying
3–4 scallions, finely chopped
1 slice fresh ginger, finely chopped
1 clove garlic, finely chopped
1 tsp sugar
1 tbsp soy sauce
1 tbsp vinegar
1 tbsp chili bean paste
2 tsp cornstarch, mixed with 2 tbsp water
1 tsp sesame oil

1 Soak the dried red chilies for 5–10 minutes, cut into small pieces. Peel the eggplant, and cut into diamond-shaped chunks.

2 Heat the oil in a wok and deep fry the eggplant for 3½–4 minutes or until soft. Remove with a slotted spoon and drain.

3 Pour off the oil and return the eggplant to the wok with the red chilies, scallions, fresh ginger and garlic. Stir a few times and add the sugar, soy sauce, vinegar and chili bean paste. Stir for 1 minute. Add the cornstarch and water mixture, blend well and garnish with sesame oil. Serve hot or cold.

Braised Eggplant

Serves 4–6
280 g (10 oz) eggplant
600 ml (1 pt) oil for deep frying
2 tbsp soy sauce
1 tbsp sugar
2 tbsp water
1 tsp sesame oil

1 Choose the long, purple variety of eggplant, rather than the large round kind, if possible. Discard the stalks and cut the eggplant into diamond-shaped chunks.

2 Heat oil in a wok until hot. Deep fry the eggplant chunks in batches until golden. Remove with a slotted spoon and drain.

3 Pour off excess oil leaving about 1 tbsp in the wok. Return the eggplant to the wok and add the soy sauce, sugar and water. Cook over fairly high heat for about 2 minutes, adding more water if necessary. Stir occasionally. When the juice is reduced to almost nothing, add the sesame oil, blend well and serve.

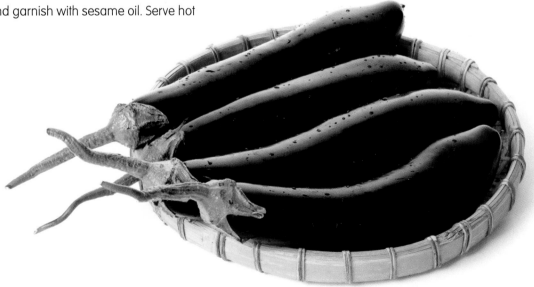

The Two Winters

Serves 4–6

380–480 g (1 lb) dried Chinese mushrooms
106 g (4 oz) winter bamboo shoots
3 tbsp vegetable oil
2 tbsp soy sauce
½ tbsp sugar
1 tsp monosodium glutamate (optional)
½ tbsp cornstarch
½ tbsp sesame oil

1 Try to select mushrooms of a uniformly small size.
   Soak them in warm water; squeeze dry and keep
   the water as mushroom stock.
2 Cut the bamboo shoots into thin slices not much
   bigger than the mushrooms.
3 Heat the oil until it smokes; stirfry the mushrooms
   and bamboo shoots for about
   1 minute; add soy sauce and sugar, stir, add
   4 tbsp mushroom stock (soaking water).
4 Bring it to a boil and cook for about 2 minutes;
   add monosodium glutamate (optional), if using,
   and cornstarch. Blend together very well, then add
   sesame oil and serve.

Colorful Beansprouts

Serves 4–6

3 pieces dried,
   spiced tofu
2 green peppers
2 red chilies
50 g (1½ oz) salted
   sour cabbage
60 g (2 oz) leeks
1 tsp sugar
4 tbsp peanut oil
1½ tsp chopped garlic
1½ tsp chopped
   fresh ginger
340 g (12 oz)
   beansprouts
2 tsp rice wine

Seasonings

2 tsp oyster sauce
1 tsp monosodium
   glutamate (optional)
2 tsp soy sauce
½ tsp salt
1 tsp sugar
¼ tsp pepper
1 tbsp cornstarch
4 tbsp stock
few drops sesame oil

1 Cut the tofu, peppers, chilies and salted sour
   cabbage into matchstick-sized shreds, and cut the
   leeks on the diagonal into 5 cm (2 in) slices. Mix
   the cabbage with 1 tsp sugar.
2 Heat 1 tsp peanut oil in a pan until very hot. Add ½
   tsp garlic and ½ tsp ginger. Stirfry the beansprouts
   for 30 seconds and set aside.
3 Heat 3 tsp peanut oil in a pan until very hot.
   Add 1 tsp garlic and 1 tsp ginger and sauté until
   fragrant. Add the grated tofu, chilies and peppers
   and stirfry over high heat for 30 seconds. Add the
   seasonings and continue to stirfry for 10 seconds.
   Sprinkle with rice wine and serve.

Ajaad Salad

Serves 4

300 ml (¾ pt) white wine vinegar
65 g (2½) oz sugar
1 tsp salt
50 g (2 oz) cucumber, quartered and sliced
50 g (2 oz) shallots, sliced
2 pieces fresh red chili, sliced into thin rounds

1 To make the dressing, mix together the white wine
   vinegar, sugar and salt. Bring to a boil and reduce
   by half. Leave to cool.
2 When ready to serve, mix all the other ingredients
   together and pour the dressing over the top.

Vegetarian Chop Suey

Serves 4–6
2 cakes of tofu
2 tbsp dried wood ear mushrooms
170 g (6 oz) broccoli or snow peas
150 g (5 oz) bamboo shoots
4–5 tbsp oil
1½ tsp salt
1 tsp sugar
1–2 scallions, finely chopped
1 tbsp light soy sauce
2 tbsp rice wine or sherry
1 tsp cornstarch mixed with
    1 tbsp cold water

1 Cut the tofu into about 24 small pieces. Soak the wood ear mushrooms in water for about 20–25 minutes, rinse them clean and discard any hard roots.
2 Cut the broccoli or snow peas and bamboo shoots into uniformly small pieces.
3 Heat a wok over high heat, add about half of the oil and wait for it to smoke. Swirl the saucepan so that its surface is well greased. Add the tofu pieces and shallow fry them on both sides until golden, then scoop them out with a slotted spoon and set them aside.
4 Heat the remaining oil and add the broccoli. Stir for about 30 seconds and then add the wood ear mushrooms, bamboo shoots and the tofu. Continue stirring for 1 minute and then add the salt, sugar, scallions, soy sauce and wine. Blend well and when the gravy starts to boil, thicken it with the cornstarch and water mixture. Serve hot.

Vegetable Casserole

Serves 4–6
2 tbsp dried wood ear mushrooms
1 tofu cake
1 tsp salt
110 g (4 oz) green beans or snow peas
110 g (4 oz) cabbage or broccoli
110 g (4 oz) baby corn or bamboo shoots
110 g (4 oz) carrots
3–4 tbsp oil
1 tsp sugar
1 tbsp light soy sauce
1 tsp cornstarch mixed with 1 tbsp cold water

1 Soak the wood ear mushrooms in water for 20–25 minutes, rinse them and discard the hard roots, if any.
2 Cut the tofu into about 12 small pieces and harden the pieces in a pot of lightly salted boiling water for 2–3 minutes. Remove and drain.
3 Trim the green beans or snow peas. Leave whole if small; cut in half if large.
4 Cut the other vegetables into thin slices or chunks.
5 Heat about half of the oil in a flameproof casserole dish or saucepan. When hot, lightly brown the tofu on both sides. Remove with a slotted spoon and set aside.
6 Heat the remaining oil and stirfry the rest of the vegetables for about 1½ minutes. Add the tofu pieces, salt, sugar and soy sauce and continue stirring to blend everything well. Cover, reduce the heat and simmer for 2–3 minutes.
7 Mix the cornstarch with water to make a smooth paste, pour it over the vegetables and stir. Increase the heat to high just long enough to thicken the gravy. Serve hot.

Braised Chinese Broccoli

Serves 4–6
450 g (1 lb) Chinese broccoli
3 tbsp oil
1 tsp salt
1 tsp sugar
1 tbsp soy sauce

1 Trim off the tough leaves and blanch the rest of the broccoli in slightly salted boiling water until soft. Remove and strain.
2 Heat a wok until hot. Add the oil and wait until it starts to smoke. Stirfry the broccoli with the salt and sugar for 1½–2 minutes. Remove and arrange neatly on a long serving dish. Pour on the soy sauce and serve.

Chinese Cabbage and Mushrooms

Serves 4–6
6–8 dried Chinese mushrooms
450 g (1 lb) Chinese cabbage leaves
6 tbsp oil
1 tsp salt
1 tsp sugar
1 tbsp soy sauce
1 tsp sesame oil

1 Soak the mushrooms in warm water for about 20 minutes. Squeeze them dry and discard the hard stalks. Keep the water. Cut each mushroom in half or into quarters depending on the size. Cut the cabbage leaves into pieces about the size of a large postage stamp.
2 Heat the oil in a wok, add the cabbage and the mushrooms and stirfry until soft. Add the salt, sugar and soy sauce and cook for 1½ minutes more. Mix in some of the mushroom water and the sesame oil.

Steamed Eggplant with Soy and Ginger

Serves 4
1 large eggplant

For the sauce:
1 clove garlic, crushed
1.25 cm (½ in) piece fresh ginger, finely grated
1 scallion, chopped
3 tbsp light soy sauce
2 tbsp white wine vinegar
1 tbsp sugar
1 tbsp sesame oil
1 red chili, chopped
1 finely chopped scallion to garnish

1   Remove the top of the eggplant, halve widthways, and then halve again lengthways. Cut the four pieces into wedges.
2   Mix the garlic, ginger, scallion, soy sauce, vinegar, sugar, sesame oil and chili in a jar, and shake well.
3   In a large pan, boil a little water under a steamer. Steam the eggplant for 15 minutes, making sure the steamer doesn't boil dry. Garnish with scallion.

"Coral" Cabbage

Serves 4–6
450 g (1 lb) Chinese white cabbage
1 tsp salt
4–5 Chinese dried mushrooms
75 g (2½ oz) bamboo shoots
4–5 dried red chilies
1 scallion
1 slice fresh ginger, peeled
2 tbsp sesame oil
2 tbsp sugar
1 tbsp soy sauce
½ tbsp rice wine or sherry
1½ tbsp vinegar

1 Parboil the cabbage; remove and drain, marinate with ½ tsp salt for 5 minutes, then squeeze dry and cut into matchbox-sized pieces; arrange on a serving dish.

2 Soak the mushrooms in warm water for 20 minutes, then squeeze dry and discard the stalks. Cut the mushrooms, bamboo shoots, red chilies, scallion and fresh ginger into thin shreds the size of matches.

3 Heat the sesame oil in a wok, stirfry all the vegetables (except the cabbage) for 2 minutes. Add the sugar, soy sauce, rice wine or sherry, vinegar and salt with about 2 tbsp water, stirfry for 1–2 minutes more and pour over the cabbage.

Hot and Sour Cabbage

Serves 4–6
680 g (1½ lb) white cabbage
5 small dried red chilies
2 tbsp soy sauce
1½ tbsp vinegar
1½ tbsp sugar
1½ tsp salt
3 tbsp oil
10 Sichuan peppercorns
1 tsp sesame oil

1 Choose a round, pale green cabbage with a firm heart—never use loose-leafed cabbage. Wash in cold water and cut the leaves into small pieces the size of a matchbox. Cut the chilies into small bits. Mix the soy sauce, vinegar, sugar and salt to make the sauce.

2 Heat the oil in a wok until it starts to smoke. Add the peppercorns and the red chilies and a few seconds later the cabbage. Stir for about 1½ minutes until the cabbage starts to go limp. Pour in the prepared sauce and continue stirring for a short while to let the sauce to blend in. Add the sesame oil just before serving. This dish is delicious both hot and cold.

Stirfried Chinese Greens

Serves 4–6
450 g (1 lb) Chinese green cabbage
1–2 slices fresh ginger, peeled
3 tbsp oil
1 tsp salt
1 tsp sugar
1 tbsp light soy sauce

1   Wash the green cabbage and trim off any tough roots. Discard any outer, discolored leaves.
2   Cut the peeled fresh ginger into small pieces.
3   Heat the oil in a wok until it smokes and swirl it to cover most of the surface. Add the fresh ginger pieces to flavor the oil. Add the greens, stir for about 1 minute and then add the salt and sugar. Continue stirring for another minute or so. Pour in the soy sauce and cook for a little longer. Serve hot. This dish is often used to add color to a meal.

Chinese Cabbage Salad

Serves 4–6
450 g (1 lb) Chinese cabbage
1 tbsp sesame oil

1   Wash the cabbage thoroughly, cut into thick slices and place in a bowl.
2   Add the soy sauce, salt, sugar and sesame oil to the cabbage. Toss well and serve.

Chinese Cabbage Casserole

Serves 4–6

450 g (1 lb) Chinese cabbage
60 g (2 oz) deep-fried tofu or 2 cakes fresh tofu
110 g (4 oz) carrots
3 tbsp oil
1 tsp salt
1 tsp sugar
2 tbsp light soy sauce
2 tbsp rice wine or sherry
1 tsp sesame oil

1 Separate the Chinese cabbage leaves; wash and cut them into small pieces. If using fresh tofu, cut each cake into about 12 pieces and fry them in a little oil until golden.

2 Peel the carrots and cut them into diamond-shaped chunks.

3 Heat the oil in a wok and stirfry the cabbage with the salt and sugar for a minute or so. Transfer it to a casserole dish and cover it with the tofu, carrots, soy sauce and rice wine or sherry. Put a lid on the pot and when it comes to the boil reduce the heat and simmer for 15 minutes.

4 Stir in the sesame oil. Add a little water if necessary and cook for a few more minutes. Serve hot.

Stirfried Mixed Vegetables

Serves 4–6

5–6 mushrooms

110 g (4 oz) carrots, sliced

110 g (4 oz) snow peas

110 g (4 oz) Chinese white cabbage

225 g (8 oz) red and yellow peppers, sliced

225 g (8 oz) broccoli florets

3 tbsp oil

1 tsp salt

1 tsp sugar

1 Chop the mushrooms, carrots, mangetout, cabbage and peppers into slices.

2 Heat the oil in a preheated wok. Add the cabbage, broccoli, carrots, peppers, snow peas and mushroom and stirfry for about 1 minute. Add the salt and sugar and stir for another minute or so with 1 tsp or more water if necessary. Do not overcook or the vegetables will lose their crunchiness. Serve hot.

Sichuan Style—Spicy Cabbage

Serves 4–6

450 g (1 lb) white cabbage
2 tsp salt
2 tbsp sesame oil
3–4 dried chilies, soaked and finely chopped
3 scallions, finely chopped
2 tsp finely chopped fresh ginger
2 tbsp sugar
60 ml (2 fl oz) water
2 tbsp vinegar

1 Discard the tough outer leaves of the cabbage and cut the tender heart into thin slices. Sprinkle with salt and leave stand for 3–4 hours. Pour off the excess water and dry the cabbage thoroughly. Place it in a bowl or a deep dish.

2 Heat the sesame oil in a pan until very hot. Add the finely chopped chilies, scallions and fresh ginger. Stir for a few seconds and then add the sugar and water. Continue stirring to dissolve the sugar. Add the vinegar and bring the mixture to a boil. Remove the saucepan from the heat and let the sauce cool; then pour it over the cabbage. Cover the bowl or plate and leave to stand for 3–4 hours before serving.

Poached Vegetables with Oyster Sauce

Serves 4–6

900 g (2 lb) Chinese greens (flowering cabbage, Chinese spinach or lettuce)
3–4 tbsp groundnut oil
3–4 tbsp oyster sauce

1 Clean the vegetables. If you are using Chinese greens, remove and discard the flowers and tough woody stems.

2 Put the vegetables into boiling water and cook for 3–5 minutes (if you are using lettuce, cook for only 1 minute). Remove and cut into 5 cm (2 in) pieces.

3 Place the vegetables on a plate, add boiling groundnut oil and oyster sauce and serve.

Chinese White Cabbage with Chilies

Serves 5–6

1¼ kg (3 lb) Chinese white cabbage
3 small red chilies
2 dried red chilies
1½ tsp Sichuan peppercorns
2 tsp salt
½ tsp sesame oil
1 tbsp vegetable oil

1 Chop the cabbage coarsely, discarding the tougher parts. Coarsely chop the chilies, discarding the seeds. Pound the peppercorns lightly. Place the cabbage in a large bowl, sprinkle evenly with the salt, chilies and peppercorns. Toss to mix. Refrigerate for 2–3 days before serving. Sprinkle the cabbage with the oils; toss well and serve.

Chinese Cabbage and Mushrooms

Serves 4–6

400 g (14 oz) Chinese cabbage	1½ tsp salt
340 g (12 oz) tinned straw mushrooms or 225 g (8 oz) fresh straw mushrooms	1 tsp sugar
	1 tbsp cornstarch mixed with 3 tbsp cold water
4 tbsp oil	120 ml (4 fl oz) milk

1 Separate and cut the cabbage leaves in half lengthways.

2 Drain the straw mushrooms. If using fresh ones, do not peel them but just wash them and trim off the roots.

3 Heat 3 tbsp oil in a hot wok, stirfry the cabbage leaves for 1 minute, add the salt and sugar, and stir for 1 minute. Remove the cabbage leaves and arrange them neatly on one side of a serving dish.

4 Heat the remaining oil until hot, then reduce the heat, add the cornstarch and water mixture and the milk and stir until thickened. Pour about half of the sauce into a jug and keep warm.

5 Add the mushrooms to the remaining sauce in the wok and heat them thoroughly over high heat. Remove the mushrooms and place them next to the cabbage leaves on the plate. Pour the sauce from the jug evenly over the cabbage and mushrooms, and serve.

Three Whites in Cream Sauce

Serves 6–8

280 g (10 oz) Chinese cabbage hearts
280 g (10 oz) tinned white asparagus spears
1–2 celery hearts
1 tbsp oil
1 scallion, cut into short lengths
2–3 slices fresh ginger, peeled
1 ½ tsp salt
1 tsp sugar
125 ml (4 fl oz) milk
1 tbsp cornstarch mixed with 3 tbsp cold water

1 Cut the cabbage hearts lengthways into thin strips. Blanch them in boiling water until they are soft, arrange them in the middle of a long serving dish with the drained asparagus.

2 Cut the celery hearts lengthways into strips, blanch until soft and add to the serving dish.

3 Heat the oil over low heat and add the scallion and fresh ginger. Discard as soon as they start turning brown. Add the milk, salt and sugar, and bring to a boil. Add the cornstarch and water mixture to thicken, stir to make it smooth and pour evenly over the vegetables. Serve hot or cold.

Mustard Greens Casserole with Ham

Serves 4–6

230 g (8 oz) mustard
greens
230 g (8 oz) cabbage
6 medium dried
black mushrooms
240 ml (8 fl oz)
groundnut oil
45 g (2 oz)
Chinese ham
250 ml (½ pt)
chicken stock

Sauce

1 tbsp oyster sauce
1 tbsp light soy sauce
1 tsp dark soy sauce
1 tsp sugar
1 tsp sesame oil
2 tsp Chinese yellow
wine

1 Chop the mustard greens and cut the cabbage into strips.
2 Soak the mushrooms in hot water for 30 minutes. Remove stems and cut each cap in half.
3 Heat the oil and fry the cabbage for 1 minute. Drain well and set aside. Fry the mustard greens for 1 minute. Drain and set aside.
4 Heat 2 tbsp oil in a clay pot or casserole dish and add the mushrooms, cabbage and mustard greens. Place the ham on top but do not mix. Add the chicken stock and bring to a boil, reduce the heat and simmer for 30–45 minutes. Add the sauce ingredients and simmer for 2 minutes. Serve in a casserole dish or Chinese clay pot.

Stuffed Green Peppers

Serves 4–6

230 g (8 oz) pork
4 x 110 g (4 oz) fish fillet
1 tsp salt
1 tbsp cornstarch
450 g (1 lb) small green peppers
2 tbsp oil
1 clove garlic, crushed
½ tbsp crushed black bean sauce
1 tbsp rice wine or sherry
2 tsp sugar
1 tbsp soy sauce

1 Finely chop the pork and fish; mix with a little salt and cornstarch.
2 Wash the green peppers; cut them in half and remove the seeds and stalks. Stuff them with the meat and fish mixture; sprinkle with a little cornstarch.
3 Heat 1 tbsp oil in a flat frying pan; put in the stuffed peppers, meat side down; fry gently for 4 minutes, adding a little more oil from time to time. When the meat side turns golden, add the crushed garlic, bean sauce, rice wine or sherry, sugar and a little water. Simmer for 2–3 minutes, then add soy sauce and a little cornstarch mixed with cold water. Serve as soon as the gravy thickens.

Stirfried Lettuce

Serves 4–6

1 large romaine lettuce
3 tbsp oil
1 tsp salt
1 tsp sugar

1 Discard the outer leaves of the lettuce. Wash the remaining leaves well and shake off the excess water. Tear the larger leaves into 2 or 3 pieces.
2 Heat the oil in a wok or large saucepan. Add the salt followed by the lettuce leaves and stir vigorously as though tossing a salad. Add the sugar and continue stirring. As soon as the leaves become slightly limp, transfer them to a serving dish and serve.

Braised Cabbage Hearts

Serves 4–6
450 g (1 lb) cabbage hearts
3–4 tbsp oil
1 tsp salt
1 tsp sugar
1 tbsp light soy sauce

1 Trim off the hard and tough roots of the cabbage, if any.
2 Parboil the cabbage in a pot of boiling water for about 1 minute and then rinse them in cold water to preserve their bright green color.
3 Heat the oil in a wok or frying pan and stirfry the cabbage with salt and sugar. Cook for about 1–1½ minutes. Add the soy sauce and a little water and braise for another minute at most. Serve hot.

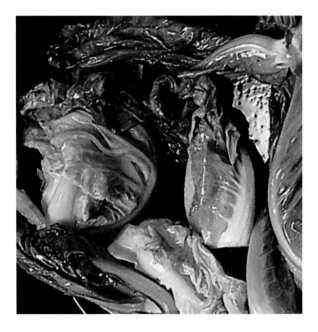

Stirfried Green and Red Peppers

Serves 3–4
1 large or 2 small green peppers, cored and seeded
1 large or 2 small red peppers, cored and seeded
3 tbsp oil
1 tsp salt
1 tsp sugar

1 Cut the peppers into small diamond-shaped pieces; if you use one or two orange peppers, the dish will be even more colorful.
2 Heat the oil in a wok or frying pan until it smokes. Spread the oil with a spatula so that the cooking surface is well greased. Add the peppers and stirfry until each piece is coated with oil. Add salt and sugar. Continue stirring for about 1 minute if you like your vegetables crunchy and crisp. If not, you can cook them for another minute or so until the skin of the peppers becomes slightly wrinkled. Add a little water if necessary during the last stage of cooking.

Green Bean and Red Pepper Salad

Serves 4–6
230 g (8 oz) green beans
1 medium or 2 small red peppers,
  cored and seeded
2 slices fresh ginger, thinly grated
1½ tsp salt
1 tsp sugar
1 tbsp sesame oil

1 Wash the green beans, snip off the ends and cut into 5 cm (2 in) lengths. Cut the red peppers into thin shreds. Blanch them both in boiling water and drain.
2 Put the green beans, red peppers and ginger into a bowl. Add the salt, sugar and sesame oil. Toss well and serve.

Stirfried Green Peppers, Tomatoes and Onions

Serves 4–6
1 large or 2 small green peppers
1 large or 2 small firm tomatoes
1 large or 2 small onions
3 tbsp oil
1 tsp salt
1 tsp sugar

1 Core and seed the green peppers and peel the onions. Cut all the vegetables into uniform slices.
2 Heat the oil in a wok and wait for it to smoke. Add the onions and stirfry for 30 seconds. Add the green peppers and continue cooking for 1 minute. Add the tomatoes, salt and sugar and cook for 1 more minute. Serve hot or cold.

Buddha's Fry

Serves 6–8

1 tbsp dried Chinese
   mushrooms
1 tbsp golden needles
   (dried tiger lily buds)
2 tbsp dried tofu
2–3 wood ear
   mushrooms
4 tbsp fresh straw
   mushrooms
50 g (2 oz)
   bamboo shoots
40 g (1½ oz) Chinese
   cabbage or celery

50 g (2 oz) snow peas
40 g (1½ oz) broccoli or
   cauliflower
60 g (2 oz) carrots
4 tbsp vegetable oil
2 tbsp soy sauce
½ tbsp sugar
1 tsp monosodium
   glutamate (optional)
160 ml (5⅓ fl oz)
   mushroom stock
1 tbsp cornstarch

1. Soak all the dry ingredients in separate bowls; cut the larger dried mushrooms into four pieces, smaller ones can be left. Cut the golden needles in half; tear the tofu into pieces roughly the same size as the wood ear mushrooms. Cut all the fresh vegetables into a roughly uniform size.

2. Heat 2 tbsp oil; stirfry the dried mushrooms, golden needles, bamboo shoots, snow peas and carrots for 1 minute, add about half of the soy sauce and sugar; stir a few more times, then add about half of the monosodium glutamate (if using) and stock. Cover and cook for 1 minute; mix in ½ tbsp cornstarch to thicken the gravy, then dish it out and keep warm.

3. Meanwhile, heat up the remaining oil and stirfry the other ingredients (the wood ear mushrooms and tofu, fresh mushrooms, Chinese cabbage and broccoli), add the remaining soy sauce, sugar, monosodium glutamate (if using) and stock. Cover and cook for about 1 minute, then add ½ tbsp cornstarch, blend well and put it on top of the first group of vegetables. Ideally these two groups of vegetables should be cooked simultaneously.

The Four Seasons

Serves 4–6

4–5 Chinese dried mushrooms (winter)

1 celery heart (summer)

85 g (2 oz) baby corn (spring)—bamboo shoots or young carrots can be used instead

3 tbsp oil

230 g (8 oz) pork fillet (autumn)

1 tsp salt

1 tsp sugar

1 tbsp soy sauce

2 tbsp rice wine or sherry

1 Soak the mushrooms in warm water for 20 minutes and discard the hard stalks. Cut the celery into small pieces. Chop the baby corn (if you are using carrots or bamboo shoots, cut into thin slices).

2 Heat 1 tbsp oil in a wok or frying pan. Stirfry the pork until the color changes. Remove the pork from the wok, add the remaining oil, and let it get hot. Put in the whole mushrooms and the other vegetables, and add the salt, sugar and pork. Stir a few times and add the soy sauce and rice wine or sherry. As soon as the juice starts to bubble, it is ready.

Pickled Vegetables

Pickling ingredients

4.8 litre (10 pt) boiled water, cooled	**Vegetables (select 4 or more):**
170 g (6 oz) salt	cucumber
60 g (2 oz) chilies	carrot
3 tsp Sichuan peppercorns	radish or turnip
	cauliflower
60 ml (2 fl oz) Chinese distilled spirit (or white rum, gin or vodka)	broccoli
	green cabbage
	white cabbage
	celery
110 g (4 oz) fresh ginger	onion
	fresh ginger
110 g (4 oz) brown sugar	leek
	scallion
	red pepper
	green pepper
	green beans
	garlic

1 Put the cold boiled water into a large, clean earthenware or glass jar. Add the salt, chilies, peppercorns, spirit, ginger and sugar.

2 Wash and trim the vegetables; peel if necessary and drain well. Put them into the jar and seal it, making sure it is airtight. Place the jar in a cool place and leave the vegetables to pickle for at least five days before serving.

3 Use a pair of clean chopsticks or tongs to pick the vegetables out of the jar. Do not allow any grease to enter the jar. You can replenish the vegetables, adding a little salt each time. If any white scum appears on the surface of the brine, add a little sugar and spirit. The longer the pickling lasts, the better.

Vegetarian Casserole

Serves 4–6

260 g (9 oz) eggplant
110 g (4 oz) green
    beans
260 g (9 oz) Chinese
    cabbage
6 medium dried
    black mushrooms
60 g (2 oz) transparent
    glass noodles
300 ml (10 fl oz)
    groundnut oil
4 pieces sweet
    dried tofu
4 slices fresh ginger

1 tsp garlic, chopped
2 tbsp fermented
    red tofu
500 ml (17 fl oz) chicken
    stock
    or water
2 pieces fried tofu
1 tsp salt
1½ tbsp cornstarch
    blended with
    1½ tbsp water
1 tsp Chinese yellow
    wine
1 tsp sesame oil

1 Cut the eggplant into long, thick strips, the green beans in half and the cabbage lengthways into quarters. Soak the black mushrooms in hot water for 30 minutes. Remove and discard the stems and cut the caps in half. Soak the noodles in hot water for 10 minutes.

2 Heat the oil in a saucepan and fry all the vegetables for 1 minute over high heat. Remove, drain and set aside. Sauté the sweet dried tofu over low heat until it is slightly browned and then remove and set aside.

3 Heat 2 tbsp oil in a clay pot or casserole dish and add the ginger and garlic. Break the fermented red tofu into pieces and add 2 tbsp to the pot, stirring over high heat to release the aroma.

4 Place all the vegetables in the clay pot and cook, stirring continuously, for 2 minutes. Add the chicken stock or water, place the fried tofu and sweet dried tofu sheets on top of the vegetables and bring to a boil. Cover the pot, lower the heat and simmer for 10 minutes.

5 Add the noodles and salt, re-cover the pot and cook for another 2 minutes over high heat. Stir in the cornstarch and water, add the Chinese yellow wine and sesame oil and serve immediately while still hot.

TOFU AND EGG DISHES

The humble soy bean is one of the key ingredients in Asian cooking. As well as being used to create of some of the most typical flavors of Asian cuisine—such as soy sauce and miso—soy beans are used to make tofu, also known as soy bean curd, an important source of protein in many cultures. Eggs, in every form, are also the main ingredient in many delicious Asian dishes.

Stirfried Tofu and Red Pepper

Serves 4

150 g (5oz) green beans, cut in half
1 tbsp sunflower oil
2 cloves garlic, minced
1.5 cm (½ in) piece fresh ginger, grated
1 red pepper, cut bite-sized pieces
300 g (11 oz) firm tofu, cut into bite-sized pieces
4 scallions, chopped
4 bok choy leaves, diced
1 tbsp rice wine, or sherry
2 tbsp black bean sauce
1 tbsp light soy sauce
1 tsp sugar

1 Blanch the green beans in a pan of water for 2 minutes and drain.
2 Heat the oil in a wok or frying pan, and stirfry the garlic and ginger for 1 minute. Add the pepper, green beans, tofu, scallions, and bok choy leaves, and stirfry for 4 to 5 minutes.
3 Add the rice wine, black bean sauce, soy sauce and sugar, then stirfry for 2 more minutes. Serve with a bowl of short-grain rice.

Fu-yung Tofu

Serves 4–6
1 cake tofu
4 egg whites
1 Romaine lettuce heart
120 ml (4 fl oz) green peas
1 scallion, finely chopped
½ tsp finely chopped fresh ginger
1 tsp salt
1 tbsp cornstarch mixed with 2 tbsp water
60 ml (2 fl oz) milk
oil for deep frying
1 tsp sesame oil

1 Cut the tofu into long, thin strips and blanch in a saucepan of salted boiling water to harden. Remove and drain.
2 Lightly beat the egg whites. Add the cornstarch mixture and milk.
3 Wash and separate the lettuce heart. If you use frozen peas, make sure they are thoroughly defrosted.
4 Wait for the tofu to cool and then coat with the egg-white mixture.
5 Heat the oil in a wok or deep fryer until it is very hot. Turn off the heat and let the oil cook a bit before adding the coated tofu. Cook for about 1–½ minutes and then scoop out with a slotted spoon and drain.
6 Pour off the excess oil, leaving about 1 tbsp in the wok. Increase the heat and stirfry the lettuce heart with a pinch of salt. When lightly done, remove and set aside on a serving dish.
7 Heat another tbsp oil in the wok and add the finely chopped scallion and fresh ginger followed by the peas, salt and a little water. When the mixture starts to boil, add the tofu strips. Blend well, add the sesame oil, and serve on the bed of lettuce heart.

Crispy-coated Coral Tofu

Serves 4–6

400 g (14 oz) fresh shrimp	**Wrappers**
60 ml (2 fl oz) pork fat	2 egg whites
1 tsp salt	3 tbsp cornstarch
½ tsp pepper	
1 tsp sesame oil	**Sweet and**
2 egg whites	**Sour Sauce**
2 tsp cornstarch	4 tsp vinegar
200 g (7 oz) tofu, crushed	3½ tsp sugar
700 ml (1½ pt) groundnut oil	2 tsp tomato ketchup
	1 tsp Worcestershire sauce
	2 tsp chili powder
	salt to taste

1 Shell and devein the prawns. Wash them in salt water, drain and pat them dry with kitchen paper. Crush with flat side of a knife.
2 Dice the pork fat into small cubes and put the shrimp, pork fat, salt, pepper, sesame oil, 2 egg whites and the cornstarch into a bowl. Stir the ingredients in one direction until they are sticky, then add the crushed tofu and continue to stir until well mixed.
3 To make the wrappers beat the egg whites and add the cornstarch, stirring and mixing thoroughly. Heat a frying pan, grease with groundnut oil and add sufficient egg-white mixture to make a wafer-thin wrappers. Peel and set aside. Repeat until all the wrappers mixture is used.
4 Flatten 1 tsp of the shrimp mixture on the palm of your hand and coat it with a little dry cornstarch. Wrap the mixture in one of the wrappers to form a roll about 3.5 x 7 cm (1½ x 3 in). Repeat until the mixture is used up.
5 Heat the groundnut oil and deep fry the rolls at a moderate heat until they are brown.
6 Serve with the spicy sweet and sour sauce.

Laksa Lemak with Tofu

Serves

300 g (12 oz) rice vermicelli

100 g (4 oz) sugarsnap peas

100 g (4 oz) beansprouts

5 tbsp sunflower oil

6 shallots, finely chopped

3 cloves garlic, finely chopped

2.5 cm (1 in) piece fresh ginger, finely chopped

3 fresh small green chilies, chopped

1 tbsp chopped lemongrass

2 tsp ground turmeric

1 tsp ground cilantro

500 ml (1 pt) chicken or vegetable broth

900 ml (2 pt) coconut milk

2 tsp sugar

2 tsp salt

400 g (14 oz) firm tofu

4 scallions, sliced diagonally

1 Soak the vermicelli in hot water for 3 minutes, then rinse and drain. Blanch the peas and beansprouts in a pan of boiling water for 2 minutes and drain.

2 Heat 3 tablespoons of the oil in a pan, add the shallots, garlic, ginger, chilies, lemongrass, turmeric and cilantro, and sauté for 3 minutes.

3 Add the broth, coconut milk, sugar and salt. Bring to the boil and simmer for 3 minutes. Add the tofu and continue to simmer for another 3 minutes.

4 Put the rice vermicelli into individual bowls and pour in the soup. Put the beansprouts, peas and tofu on top of the noodles. Pour the soup over all, garnish with sliced scallions, and serve.

Sichuan Tofu

Serves 4–6

2 tbsp dried wood ear mushrooms
3 cakes tofu
1–2 leeks or 2–3 scallions
3 tbsp oil
1 tsp salted black beans
1 tbsp chili bean paste
2 tbsp rice wine or sherry
1 tbsp light soy sauce
1 tsp cornstarch mixed with 1 tbsp cold water
freshly ground Sichuan pepper

1   Soak the wood ear mushrooms in water for 20–25 minutes, rinse them clean, discard any hard roots and then drain. If you use dried mushrooms, they should be soaked in hot or warm water for at least 30–35 minutes. Squeeze them dry, throw out the hard stalks and cut into small pieces, retaining the water for later use.
2   Cut the tofu into 1.5 cm (½ in) cubes. Blanch them in a saucepan of boiling water for 2–3 minutes, remove and drain.
3   Cut the leeks or scallions into short lengths.
4   Heat the oil in a hot wok until it smokes and stirfry the leeks or scallions and the wood ear mushrooms or mushrooms for about 1 minute. Add the salted black beans, crush them with the spatula and blend well. Now add the tofu, the chili bean paste, rice wine or sherry and soy sauce and continue stirring to blend. Add a little water and cook for 3–4 more minutes. Finally add the cornstarch and water mixture to thicken the gravy. Serve hot with freshly ground Sichuan pepper as a garnish.

Tofu à la Maison

Serves 4–6

4 cakes tofu
110 g (4 oz) pork
30 g (1½ oz) leeks
5–6 dried red chilies
oil for deep frying
1 tbsp rice wine or sherry
1 tbsp soy sauce
2 tbsp crushed yellow bean sauce
½ tsp sesame oil

1   Split each cake of tofu into three or four thin slices crossways, then cut each slice diagonally into two triangles.
2   Cut the pork into small, thin slices; diagonally cut the leek into chunks; cut the dried red chilies into small pieces.
3   Heat up the oil; deep fry the tofu pieces for about 2 minutes; remove and drain.
4   Pour out the excess oil, leaving about 1 tbsp in the wok. Put in the pork and red chilies, stir; add rice wine or sherry, soy sauce, tofu, leek and crushed bean sauce; cook for about 3 minutes. Add sesame oil and serve.

Basic Steamed Egg and Fancy Steamed Eggs

Serves 4–6

2 eggs	**Optional extras**
300 ml (10 fl oz) good stock, or water	2–3 tbsp grated crab meat or shrimp
salt and pepper to taste	1–2 tbsp ham, chopped
1 tbsp soy sauce	1–2 tbsp peas
1 tbsp finely chopped scallion	

1 The most basic Chinese steamed egg dish consists of no more than 2 eggs mixed with 300 ml (10 fl oz) stock or water in a dish with seasoning added and cooked in a steamer for about 15 minutes, or until the custard has set. It is then topped with a spoonful of soy sauce and a scattering of chopped scallion.

2 A more elaborate version consists of using the stock, perhaps with a little grated crabmeat or other shellfish added. After steaming, the top of the custard should be set and firm enough so that more seafood can be arranged on top, together with some chopped ham and peas. The dish is then returned to the steamer for 3–4 more minutes. After the second steaming, a large pinch of chopped scallion is sprinkled over the top. When cooking this dish, never use too many eggs, as this will cause the custard to become hard after steaming.

Stirfried Chinese Omelet with Tomatoes

Serves 4–6

4–5 eggs
½ tsp salt
pepper to taste
1 medium onion
3 medium tomatoes
4–5 tbsp vegetable oil
1 tsp sesame oil
1½ tbsp scallion, finely chopped
1½ tbsp soy sauce

1 Break the eggs into a bowl with the salt and pepper and beat lightly with a fork. Peel and finely slice the onion. Cut each tomato into 8 segments.

2 Heat the vegetable oil in a wok or frying pan. When hot, gently stirfry the onion for about 30 seconds, then add the tomatoes. Spread evenly over the bottom of the span. Pour over the beaten egg and allow to flow over the base of the pan. When the edges of the egg have begun to set, gently turn and stir several times, allowing any uncooked liquid to come in contact with the surface of the pan. Sprinkle on the sesame oil and arrange the omelet on a heated dish. Sprinkle over the chopped scallion, with extra scallion shreds if desired, and soy sauce, and serve.

RICE AND NOODLES

Rice is the staple food of Asia and every country has its own specialty rice dishes; indeed, different rice varieties are favored in different countries— basmati rice in India and Pakistan, glutinous rice in China and Japan, and fragrant rice in Thailand and Vietnam. Noodles are just as widespread and can be made from either rice flour, wheat flour, buckwheat or mung bean starch, depending on regional variations in the crops grown.

Boiled Rice

Serves 4–6
200 g (6 oz) long-grain rice
600 ml (1 pt) water

1   Wash and rinse the rice in cold water until
    clean. Bring the water to a boil in a saucepan
    over high heat. Add the washed rice and bring
    back to a boil. Stir the rice with a spoon to prevent
    it from sticking to the bottom of the saucepan and
    then cover the saucepan tightly with a lid and
    reduce the heat to very low. Cook gently for
    15–20 minutes.

Rice Gruel or Congee

Serves 4–6
315 g (10 oz) long-grain white rice
2.5 ml (5 pt) water

1   Wash and rinse the rice, drain well. Place in a
    deep heavy pot or saucepan and add the water.
    Bring to a boil, reduce the heat and simmer
    very gently, uncovered, for 30 minutes, stirring
    occasionally. By this time, the rice will be fairly thick
    and porridgy. Serve accompanied by pickled or
    salted foods.

Cook's tip
Congee, rather like a rice porridge, is popularly eaten
for breakfast. It is filling but bland, and often enlivened
with strong-tasting savory accompaniments such
as salted fish or shredded dried meat.

Yin and Yang Rice

Serves 4–6
4 x 230 g (½ lb)
 chicken breast
260 g (9 oz) shrimp,
 shelled and deveined
350 ml (12 fl oz)
 groundnut oil
1 tbsp fresh
 ginger, grated
2 eggs, beaten
160 g (5 oz) cold plain
 cooked rice
2 tbsp light soy sauce
300 ml (10 fl oz) chicken
 stock (see page 152)
30 g (1½ oz) peas
1 tsp salt
½ tsp fresh ginger,
 chopped
1 tsp garlic, chopped

Marinade
1 egg white
1 tbsp cornstarch
1 tsp sesame oil
1 tsp salt

White Sauce
8 tbsp chicken stock
2 tbsp milk
1 tbsp cornstarch
1 tsp salt

Red Sauce
1½ tbsp tomato
 ketchup
8 tbsp chicken stock
1 tbsp cornstarch
1 tsp sugar
1 tbsp light soy sauce

1 Mix the marinade ingredients in a bowl. Slice the chicken breast thinly. and add to half of the marinade. Set aside.

2 Clean the shrimp and pat them dry. Mix them with the other half of the marinade and refrigerate for 30 minutes.

3 Heat 50 ml (2 fl oz) oil in a saucepan and add 1 tbsp grated ginger. Add the beaten eggs and, when the eggs are partly set, add the rice. Stirfry for 2 minutes, breaking up the egg with a spatula. Add the soy sauce and chicken stock and keep on stirfrying for 3 minutes. Transfer to a large dish.

4 Heat the oil in a saucepan. Add the shrimp, stirring to separate. Remove and set aside. Add the chicken to the oil, again stirring to separate. Remove and set aside. Cook the peas in 8 tbsp water with 1 tsp salt for 5 minutes. Drain and set aside.

5 Heat 1 tbsp oil in the saucepan and add ½ tsp garlic. When it starts to smell, return the shrimp and peas to the saucepan. Add the white sauce ingredients and bring to a boil. Pour over one half of the dish of fried rice, using an S-shaped piece of foil to keep the sauce to one side of the dish.

6 Heat 1 tbsp oil in the saucepan and add ½ tsp ginger and 1 tsp garlic; when it starts to smell, return the chicken to the saucepan. Add the red sauce and bring to a boil. Pour over the fried rice on the other side of the foil. Remove the foil and serve.

Cook's tip
The two different rices should be presented together to form the Taoist yin and yang symbol.

Ten-variety Fried Rice

Serves 4–6
215 g (7 oz) rice
110 g (4 oz) shrimp
110 g (4 oz) cooked ham or pork
2 scallions
3 eggs
½ tsp salt
2 tbsp oil
110 g (4 oz) peas
2 tbsp soy sauce

1   Wash the rice in cold water, then cover it with more cold water so that there is about 2.5 cm (1 in) of water above the surface of the rice in the saucepan.
2   Bring it to a boil; stir to prevent it sticking to the bottom of the saucepan. Replace the lid tightly and reduce the heat as low as possible. Cook for about 15–20 minutes.
3   Peel the shrimp and dice the ham or pork into small cubes the size of the peas. Finely chop the scallions. Beat the eggs with a little salt; heat up about 1 tbsp oil and make an omelet; set aside to cool. Heat the remaining oil, stirfry the scallions, followed by the shrimp, ham or pork, and peas; stir, adding a little salt, then add the cooked rice and soy sauce. When all the ingredients are mixed well, add the omelet, breaking it into little pieces. When everything is mixed it is ready to serve.

Fried Rice, Chiu Chow Style

Serves 3–4
110 g (4 oz) Chinese kale, stem only
4 tbsp groundnut oil
2 tbsp grated fresh ginger
110 g (4 oz) shrimp, shelled and deveined
2 eggs, beaten
160 g (5 oz) cold plain cooked rice
2 tbsp shrimp or fish sauce
600 ml (1 pt) chicken stock (see page 152)

1   Dice the stems of the Chinese kale into small pieces.
2   Heat the oil in a frying pan and add the grated ginger, shrimp and Chinese kale, stirfrying them for 1 minute.
3   Add the eggs (beaten for 10 seconds) and, when they are partly set, add the cold plain rice. Stirfry over very high heat. Scramble the eggs, breaking them into tiny pieces with your spoon or spatula.
4   Add the shrimp or fish sauce and chicken stock and stirfry over reduced heat for 3–5 more minutes. Serve.

Yanchow Fried Rice

Serves 4–6
250 g (9 oz) cold plain cooked rice
1 medium red pepper
40 g (2 oz) beansprouts
90 g (3 oz) fresh or frozen medium or
    large shrimp
60–90 g (2–3 oz) tinned straw mushrooms or
    110 g (4 oz) fresh button mushrooms
1 medium zucchini
2½ tbsp vegetable oil
2 tbsp sweetcorn
90 g (3 oz) fresh or frozen small shrimp
20 g (¾ oz) lard or butter
½ tbsp light soy sauce

1 Cut the red pepper into 7.5 mm (¼ in) pieces.
   Wash and dry the beansprouts. Cut each shrimp
   into 2–3 pieces. If using button mushrooms,
   quarter them. Cut the zucchini into 8 sections, then
   further divide into quarters.
2 Heat the oil in a wok or frying pan. When hot,
   stirfry the pepper, mushrooms, beansprouts,
   zucchini, corn kernels and all the shrimp over high
   heat for 1½ minutes. Add the lard and light soy
   sauce and continue to stirfry over medium heat for
   1½ minutes. Pour the contents into the saucepan
   containing the fried rice. Reduce the heat to low,
   turn and stir together for 30 seconds.

Fukien Crab Rice

Serves 6–8
315 (10 oz) cooked   30 g (1 oz) lard
    glutinous rice   1 tsp salt
315 (10 oz) cooked   180 ml (6 fl oz) stock
    long-grain rice   1 chicken stock cube
230–340 (8–12 oz)   2 tbsp tomato paste
    young leeks   1 tsp paprika
3 slices fresh ginger   1 tbsp light soy sauce
2 cloves garlic   160 ml (5⅓ oz) rice
2 medium crabs,   wine or sherry
    about 1.3 kg (3 lb)   1 tbsp cornstarch
160 ml (5⅓ fl oz)   blended with
    vegetable oil   2 tbsp water

1 Place the glutinous rice in a bowl over a saucepan
   of water. Bring to a boil and simmer gently for 15
   minutes. Add this rice to the cooked long-grain
   rice and mix together.
2 Clean and cut the leeks on the diagonal into
   2.5 cm (1 in) sections. Grate the ginger. Coarsely
   chop the garlic. Chop each crab through the shell
   into 12 pieces, cracking the claws with the side of
   the chopper. Discard the dead men's fingers.
3 Heat the oil in a wok or large frying pan. When
   very hot, add the crab pieces and turn them
   around in the hot oil for 3 minutes. Drain. Pour
   away the oil to use for other purposes, leaving
   2 tbsp. Add the lard and reheat the pan. When
   hot, stirfry the ginger and garlic over medium
   heat for 15 seconds. Add the leeks and salt and
   stirfry for 1 minute. Pour in the stock and sprinkle
   in the crumbled stock cube, then add the tomato
   paste, paprika, soy sauce and sherry. Bring to
   a boil, stirring, and return the crab pieces to the
   saucepan. Cook over medium heat for 3 minutes.
   Add the blended cornstarch, turn and stir a few
   times until thickened.
4 Place the mixed rice into a medium two-handled
   wok with a lid, or a large flameproof casserole
   dish. Pour the crab and leek mixture over the rice.
   Place the wok or casserole dish over low heat,
   cover and cook gently for 5 minutes.

Vegetarian Special Fried Rice

Serves 4–6

4–6 dried Chinese mushrooms
1 green pepper, cored and seeded
1 red pepper, cored and seeded
90 g (3 oz) bamboo shoots
2 eggs
2 scallions, finely chopped
2 tsp salt
4–5 tbsp oil
950 g (2 lbs) cooked rice
1 tbsp light soy sauce (optional)

1 Soak the dried mushrooms in warm water for 25–30 minutes, squeeze dry and discard the hard stalks. Cut into small cubes.

2 Cut the green and red peppers and the bamboo shoots into small cubes. Lightly beat the eggs with about half of the scallions and a pinch of the salt.

3 Heat about 2 tbsp oil in a wok, add the beaten eggs and scramble until set. Remove.

4 Heat the remaining oil. When hot, add the rest of the scallions followed by all the vegetables and stirfry until each piece is covered with oil. Add the cooked rice and salt and stir to separate each grain of rice. Finally add the soy sauce, blend everything together and serve.

Shanghai Vegetable Rice

Serves 5–6

315 g (10 oz) long-grain rice
450 g (1 lb) cabbage or greens
1½ tbsp dried shrimp
about 230 g (8 oz) Chinese sausages
2 tbsp vegetable oil
1½ tsp lard
1½ tsp salt

1 Wash and measure the rice. Simmer in the same volume of water for 6 minutes. Remove from the heat and leave to stand, covered, for 7–8 minutes. Wash and dry the cabbage. Chop into 3.5 x 7 cm (1½ x 3 in) pieces, removing the tougher stalks. Soak the dried shrimp in hot water to cover for 7–8 minutes, then drain. Cut the sausages on the diagonal into 2.5 cm (1 in) sections.

2 Heat the oil and lard in a deep saucepan. When hot, stirfry the shrimp for 30 seconds. Add the cabbage and toss and turn for 1½ minutes until well coated with oil. Sprinkle the cabbage with the salt. Pack in the rice. Push pieces of sausage into the rice. Add 4–5 tbsp water down the side of the saucepan. Cover and simmer very gently for about 15 minutes. Transfer to a heated serving dish.

Beijing Ja Chiang Mein Noodles

Serves 4–6

1 medium onion
2 slices fresh root ginger
2 cloves garlic
4 scallions
15 cm (6 in) piece of cucumber
450 g (1 lb) wheat-flour noodles (like spaghetti)
4 tbsp vegetable oil
230 g (8 oz) pork mince
½ tsp salt
1 tbsp yellow bean paste
1 tbsp soy sauce
4 tbsp good stock
1 tbsp cornstarch blended with 3 tbsp water

1 Coarsely chop the onion, ginger and garlic. Cut the scallions into 6 cm (2½ in) sections (dividing the larger stalks in half or quarters. Cut the cucumber into matchstick-sized shreds. Place the noodles in a saucepan of boiling water and simmer for 8–10 minutes. Drain. Rinse the noodles under cold running water to separate them.

2 Heat the oil in a wok or large frying pan. When hot, stirfry the onion and ginger for 1 minute. Add the garlic and pork and stirfry over medium heat for 3 minutes. Add the salt, yellow bean paste and soy sauce. Stir and cook for 3 minutes. Mix in the stock and continue to cook for 3 more minutes. Pour in the blended cornstarch, stirring until thickened.

3 Reheat the noodles by dipping them in boiling water for 15 seconds, then drain thoroughly. Arrange them on a large heated serving dish. Pour the sauce into the center of the noodles. Arrange the grated cucumber and scallion sections on either side of the sauce.

Vegetarian Noodles in Soup

Serves 4–6

125 g (4½ oz) water chestnuts
110 g (4 oz) straw mushrooms
110 g (4 oz) ginko nuts
3 tbsp oil
1 tsp salt
1 tsp sugar
1 tbsp light soy sauce
230 g (8 oz) egg vermicelli or noodles
1 tsp sesame oil

1 Drain the ingredients if they are canned, and cut the water chestnuts into thin slices. The straw mushrooms and ginko nuts can be left whole.

2 Heat the oil in a wok or frying pan. When it starts to smoke, add the vegetables and stirfry for a few seconds. Add the salt, sugar and soy sauce and continue stirring. When the gravy begins to boil, reduce the heat and let it simmer gently.

3 Cook the noodles in boiling water. Drain and place them in a large serving bowl. Pour a little of the cooking water into the bowl—just enough to half cover the noodles. Then quickly pour the entire contents of the wok or frying pan over the top. Garnish with the sesame oil and serve hot.

Sesame Pork and Black Mushrooms with Noodles

Serves 6–8
60 g (2 oz) pork
1 medium dried black mushroom
1 Chinese cabbage
450 g (1 lb) dried egg noodles
2 tbsp groundnut oil

Sauce
2 tbsp sesame paste
1 tbsp fish or shrimp sauce
1 tsp sugar
1 tsp Chinese yellow wine
2 tbsp cornstarch
240 ml (8 fl oz) chicken stock (see page 152)

1   Cut the pork into matchstick-sized shreds. Soak the black mushroom in hot water for 30 minutes. Remove and discard the stem and chop the cap finely. Set aside. Chop the celery into small pieces.

2   Bring 2.5 l (5 pt) water to a boil. Add the noodles, stirring to separate, and cook for 3 minutes. Transfer the noodles to a large saucepan of cold water. Return the noodles to boiling water and cook for 1 minute. Drain and place in a large bowl or on a plate. Set aside.

3   Heat 2 tbsp groundnut oil in a frying pan. When hot, add the pork and stirfry for 1 minute over high heat. Add the mushrooms and celery, and continue to cook for 30 seconds.

4   Add the sauce ingredients and bring to a boil. Return the noodles to the frying pan, stirring, and cook for another 30 seconds.

5   Transfer the noodles to a serving plate first, and place the pork, mushroom and celery on top as a garnish. Pour the sauce over them and serve.

Fried Rice Noodles

Serves 6–8
450 g (1 lb) rice noodles
2 tbsp dried shrimp
3–4 small dried Chinese mushrooms
40 g (1½ oz) chopped pork
40 g (1½ oz) bamboo shoots
1 leek
1 celery stalk
4 tbsp oil
1 tsp salt
4 tbsp stock
2 tbsp light soy sauce

1   Soak the rice noodles in warm water until soft; soak the dried shrimp and mushrooms. Cut the pork, bamboo shoots and leek into matchstick-sized shreds.

2   Stirfry the pork, bamboo shoots, shrimp, celery and leeks in a little hot oil; add salt and stock; cook for about 2 minutes, remove.

3   Heat the remaining oil; stirfry the rice noodles for 2–3 minutes; add the other cooked ingredients and soy sauce; stir for 2 more minutes until there is no juice left at all; serve hot.

Chow Mein—Fried Noodles

Serves 3–4

1 tbsp dried tofu skin sticks
1 tbsp dried tiger lily buds
50 g (2 oz) bamboo shoots
110 g (4 oz) spinach or any other greens
230 g (8 oz) dried egg noodles
3–4 tbsp oil
2 scallions, finely chopped
2 tbsp light soy sauce
1 tsp salt
2 tsp sesame oil

1 Soak the dried vegetables overnight in cold water or in hot water for at least an hour. When soft, thinly grate both the tofu skins and tiger lily buds.

2 Grate the bamboo shoots and spinach leaves into thin strips.

3 Cook the noodles in a saucepan of boiling water according to the instructions on the packet. Depending on the thickness of the noodles, this should take 5 minutes or so. Freshly made noodles will take only about half that time.

4 Heat about half of the oil in a wok or frying pan. While waiting for it to smoke, drain the noodles in a strainer. Add them with about half of the scallions and the soy sauce to the wok and stirfry. Do not overcook, or the noodles will become soggy. Remove and place them on a serving dish.

5 Add the rest of the oil to the wok. When hot, add the other scallions and stir a few times. Then add all the vegetables and continue stirring. After 30 seconds or so, add the salt and the remaining soy sauce together with a little water if necessary. As soon as the gravy starts to boil, add the sesame oil and blend everything well. Place the mixture on top of the fried noodles as a dressing.

Beef, Celery and Noodle Soup

Serves 4–6

230 g (8 oz) Chinese celery

230 g (8 oz) Chinese white chives or the white part of leeks

560 g (1¼ lb) thick noodles

550 ml (1 pt) chicken stock, boiling (see page 152)

4 tbsp groundnut oil

560 g (1¼ lb) ground beef

2 tsp chopped scallions

2 tsp chopped fresh ginger

2 tsp chopped Sichuan pickle

1 tbsp dark soy sauce

2 tsp chili oil

2 tsp Sichuan peppercorn powder

4 tbsp chicken stock

1 Chop the celery and white chives or leeks into shavings. Set aside.

2 Bring 2½ l (5 pt) water to a boil and add the noodles. Reduce the heat to medium and cook for 5–6 minutes. Transfer the noodles to a large saucepan of cold water, stirring to keep them separate. Drain the noodles and return them to a saucepan of boiling water and cook for 2 more minutes. Test with your fingers to see if they are cooked: they should be firm but easy to break. When they are cooked, remove and drain them and divide them among four or six bowls.

3 Add 500 ml (17 fl oz) boiling chicken stock to the noodles in the bowls. Heat the oil in a saucepan, add the beef and stirfry quickly over high heat. Add the chopped celery and chives and, continuing to stir, cook for 30 seconds.

4 Add the remaining ingredients, including an additional 4 tbsp chicken stock, stir and bring the contents to a boil. Ladle over each bowl of noodles and serve.

E-fu Noodles with Pork and Mushrooms

Serves 4–6

60 g (2 oz) pork fillet

1 tsp cornstarch

2 medium dried black mushrooms

110 g (4 oz) chives

700 ml (1½ pt) boiling water

110 g (4 oz) e-fu noodles

3–4 tbsp groundnut oil

1 tbsp fresh ginger, grated

Sauce

1 tbsp oyster sauce

1 tbsp light soy sauce

1 tsp dark soy sauce

1 tsp sesame oil

½ tsp sugar

1 Mix the sauce ingredients together in a bowl. Cut the pork into matchstick-sized shreds and add 1 tbsp of the mixed sauce and 1 tsp cornstarch. Mix well and set aside.

2 Soak the black mushrooms in hot water for 30 minutes. Remove and discard the stems and cut the caps into shreds. Set aside. Cut the chives into 3.5 cm (1½ in) pieces and set aside. Bring the water to a boil and add the noodles. Parboil until soft. Remove, drain and dry the noodles with paper towels.

3 Heat 3–4 tbsp oil in frying pan. Add the ginger and pork and stirfry for 1 minute. Add the mushrooms, stir and continue to cook for another minute. Return the noodles to the saucepan and add the rest of the sauce. Stir and mix the ingredients together, simmering over medium heat until all the water is absorbed by the noodles.

4 Sprinkle the chives over the noodles and cook for 30 seconds. Transfer to a plate and serve immediately.

Shrimp and Noodle Balls

Makes 15
110 g (4 oz) Chinese rice vermicelli (*beehoon*)
230 g (8 oz) peeled shrimp
½ tsp sugar
60 g (2 oz) pork fat
few slices fresh root ginger
salt and pepper
oil for deep frying

1   Crush the *beehoon* finely and leave in a dry place.
Mince the shrimp in a food processor and sprinkle
with sugar. Mince the pork fat with fresh ginger,
add the shrimp with seasoning and bind together.
Use wetted hands to form into even, bite-sized
balls. Chill well, and roll in crushed *beehoon* just
before frying in hot oil. Cook for about 3–4 minutes
until cooked through, or steam in a bamboo
steamer over hot water for 30 minutes.

Pork and Chinese Cabbage with Noodles

Serves 4–6
560 g (1¼ lb) Chinese cabbage
110 g (4 oz) mung bean noodles
4 tbsp dried shrimp
40 g (1½ oz) pork fillet, chopped
3–4 tbsp groundnut oil
1 litre (2 pt) chicken stock (see page 152)
1 tsp salt
2 tsp Chinese yellow wine

Seasonings
1 tsp salt
2 tsp cornstarch
½ tsp sesame oil
½ tsp sugar
3–4 slices fresh root ginger

1   Cut the Chinese cabbage into 5 cm (2 in) pieces.
Soak the mung bean noodles and the dried
shrimp in water for about 15 minutes until they
are softened. Shred the fillet of pork and mix
the meat with the seasoning ingredients. Heat
3–4 tbsp oil in a clay pot or a wok and add the
ginger slices and grated fillet of pork, stirring to
separate. Then add the dried shrimp.

2   Add the cabbage, stir and mix well. Pour in the
chicken stock and bring the contents to a boil.
Reduce the heat and simmer for 15 minutes. Add
the mung bean noodles and simmer for another
2–3 minutes. Finally add salt and Chinese yellow
wine and serve.

Beggars' Noodles

Serves 4–6

3 scallions
3 tbsp soy sauce
3 tbsp wine vinegar
500 g (1 lb) wheat-flour noodles

Sauce

3 tbsp peanut butter
2 tbsp sesame paste
3 tbsp sesame oil

1 Coarsely chop or shred the scallions. Mix the soy sauce and vinegar together. Mix the peanut butter, sesame paste and sesame oil together for the sauce.

2 Place the noodles in a saucepan of boiling water and simmer for 10 minutes, or spaghetti for about 10–12 minutes. Drain.

3 Divide the hot noodles into 4–6 heated large rice bowls. Sprinkle evenly with the scallions. Add a large spoonful of the peanut butter and sesame mixture to each bowl of noodles. Pour 1 tbsp soy sauce and vinegar mixture over the contents of each bowl.

SOUPS

In Asian countries soup is sometimes served as a separate course, just as in the West. However, more often than not, soup either accompanies a meal or is eaten as a meal in itself. When served with other dishes, the soup is usually a light one; it's meant to be drunk along with the rest of the meal. Thick soups, packed with ingredients, are more likely to be served as a meal in their own right—most often at lunchtime.

Fresh Poultry Stock

Serves 12
1½ kg (3–4 lb) chicken or duck
2 l (4 pt) water
3–4 slices fresh root ginger

1 Remove the breast and legs from the chicken or duck. Cover the remaining bird in water and boil for 20 minutes. Remove from the heat and add the remaining cold water, skim the scum off the surface of the liquid.
2 Add ginger and continue to simmer gently for about 1½ hours. After an hour remove the bird from the stock.
3 Grind the leg and the breast meat separately. Add the leg meat back to the stock and simmer for 10 minutes, then add the breast meat and simmer for 5 minutes.
4 Strain the stock through a fine sieve or muslin.

Bacon and Bamboo Shoot Soup

Serves 4–6
100 g (4 oz) unsmoked fatty bacon in one piece
175 g (6 oz) bamboo shoot tips
600 ml (1 pt) water
1 tbsp rice wine or sherry
50 g (2 oz) seasonal greens
½ tsp monosodium glutamate (optional)
1 tsp salt
1 tbsp lard

1 Dice the bacon into small cubes and the bamboo shoot tips into small triangles.
2 Bring water to a boil; put in the bacon and bamboo shoots at the same time; add wine or sherry, then reduce heat and simmer for 10 minutes. Add the greens, monosodium glutamate (if using) and salt; increase heat to high again and when the soup starts to boil put in the lard and serve.

Deep-fried Tofu and Wood Ear Mushroom Soup

Serves 4–6
50 g (2 oz) fresh tofu cakes
15 g (½ oz) wood ear mushrooms
600 ml (1 pt) water
1 tsp salt
1 tbsp light soy sauce
1 scallion, finely chopped
1 tsp sesame oil

1 Cut the tofu into approximately 20 small cubes and deep fry them vegetable oil. Cut them in half
2 Soak the wood ear mushrooms in water until soft (about 20–25 minutes) and rinse until clean.
3 Bring the water to a boil in a wok or large pot. Add the tofu, wooden ear mushrooms and the salt. When the soup starts to boil again, add the soy sauce and cook for about 1 minute. Garnish with scallion and sesame oil. Serve hot.

Beansprout Soup

Serves 4–6
230 g (8 oz) fresh beansprouts
1 small red pepper, cored and seeded
2 tbsp oil
2 tsp salt
600 ml (1 pt) water
1 scallion, finely chopped

1   Wash the beansprouts in cold water, discarding the husks and other pieces that float to the surface. It is not necessary to trim each sprout. Thinly shred the pepper.
2   Heat a wok or large pot, add the oil and wait for it to smoke. Add the beansprouts and red pepper and stir a few times. Add the salt and water. When the soup starts to boil, garnish with scallion and serve hot.

Pickled Cabbage and Chicken Soup

Serves 4–6
260 g (9 oz) pickled cabbage
260 g (9 oz) chicken breast
1 l (2 pt) chicken stock (see page 152)
300 ml (10 fl oz) water
4 slices fresh root ginger

Marinade
1 egg white
1 tbsp light soy sauce
½ tsp sesame oil
1 tsp cornstarch

1   Soak the pickled cabbage in salted water for 2 hours. Rinse under cold running water, squeezing several times. Cut into strips. Cut the chicken breast meat into thin slices. Mix the marinade, add the chicken and set aside.
2   Put the chicken stock, water, ginger and cabbage in a pot and bring to a boil. Reduce the heat and simmer for 15 minutes. Bring 500 ml (17 fl oz) water to a boil. Add the chicken slices, stir to separate and remove immediately. Drain the chicken and transfer the pieces to the soup in the pot. Simmer for 3 minutes and serve.

Chicken and Shrimp Ball Soup

Serves 4–6
230 g (8 oz) uncooked shrimp
50 g (2 oz) chopped pork fat
50 g (2 oz) chopped chicken breast
50 g (2 oz) chopped cooked ham
½ cucumber
1½ tbsp cornstarch
2 egg whites
1 slice fresh root ginger, peeled and finely grated
2 tbsp rice wine or sherry
2 tsp salt
1 litre (2 pt) stock

1 Shell the shrimp and finely grind into a pulp. Mince the pork fat and chicken breast meat. Finely chop the ham. Slice the cucumber thinly.
2 Mix ½ tbsp cornstarch with 4 tbsp water, add the ground chicken breast and 1 egg white, blend well. This is the chicken purée.
3 Mix together the shrimp, pork fat, the remaining cornstarch, egg white, root ginger, 1 tbsp rice wine or sherry and 1 tsp salt; blend well.
4 Bring the stock to a boil, then reduce the heat and put in the shrimp and pork fat mixture made into small balls about the size of walnuts. Increase the heat to bring it back to a boil. Now add the remaining salt and rice wine or sherry, then reduce the heat again and simmer gently for about 10 minutes. Stir the chicken purée and add it to the soup, stirring all the time so it does not form into lumps.
5 Add the ham and cucumber; turn up the heat to bring to a rapid boil; serve in a large bowl.

Chinese Cabbage Soup

Serves 4–6
260 g (9 oz) Chinese cabbage
3–4 dried Chinese mushrooms, soaked in warm water for 30 minutes
2 tbsp oil
2 tsp salt
1 tbsp rice wine or sherry
1 l (2 pt) water
1 tsp sesame oil

1 Wash the cabbage and cut it into thin slices. Squeeze the soaked mushrooms dry. Discard the hard stalks and cut the mushrooms into small pieces. Reserve the water in which the mushrooms have been soaked.
2 Heat a wok or large pot until hot, add oil and wait for it to smoke. Add the cabbage and mushrooms. Stir a few times and then add the salt, wine, water and also the water in which mushrooms were soaked. Bring to a boil, add the sesame oil and serve.

Beijing Sliced Fish Pepperpot Soup

Serves 4–6

230 g (8 oz) white fish fillets
2 tsp salt
1 tbsp cornstarch
1 egg white
2 slices fresh root ginger
1 clove garlic
2 scallions
vegetable oil for deep frying
1 litre (2 pt) chicken stock (see page 152)
¼ tsp monosodium glutamate (optional)
3 tbsp wine vinegar
½ tsp pepper

1 Cut the fish into 3.5 x 2 cm (1½ x ¾ in) slices. Dust with the 1½ tsp salt and the cornstarch, and wet with the egg white. Finely chop the ginger and garlic. Coarsely chop the scallions.

2 Heat the oil in a wok or deep fryer. When hot, lightly fry the coated fish for 1 minute. Remove and drain. Bring the stock to a boil in the wok or saucepan. Add the ginger, garlic, remaining salt and monosodium glutamate, if using, and bring back to a boil for 1 minute. Add the fish, vinegar and pepper and simmer for 3–4 minutes. Pour into a heated serving dish, sprinkle with scallions and serve.

Crabmeat Soup

Serves 4–6

170–200 g (6–7 oz) crabmeat, fresh or frozen
2 slices fresh root ginger
2 scallions
1 cake fresh tofu
230 g (8 oz) young spinach
2 tbsp vegetable oil
1 l (2 pt) stock
1 chicken stock cube
1 tsp salt
pepper to taste
2 tbsp cornstarch blended with 5 tbsp water

1 Flake the crabmeat, thawing first if necessary. Coarsely chop the ginger. Cut the scallions into 1.25 cm (½ in) shreds. Cut the tofu into cubes. Wash the spinach, removing any tough stems or discolored leaves.

2 Heat the oil in a wok or saucepan. When hot, stirfry the ginger and scallions for 30 seconds. Add the crabmeat and stirfry for 15 seconds. Pour in the stock. Add the crumbled stock cube and the salt and pepper. Bring to a boil, stirring. Add the spinach and tofu. Bring contents to a boil again, stirring, then simmer gently for 2 minutes. Stir in the blended cornstarch and cook until thickened.

Hot and Sour Soup

Serves 4–6
110 g (4 oz) lean pork
45 g (2 oz) tinned bamboo shoots
4 medium dried Chinese mushrooms
1 tbsp carrot
1–2 fresh tofu cakes
1 egg
2 scallions
1.2 l (2½ pt) good stock
3 tbsp fresh or frozen shrimp
1 tsp salt
2 stock cubes
2 tbsp peas
1 tsp sesame oil

Hot and Sour Mixture
2 tbsp soy sauce
3 tbsp vinegar
2 tbsp cornstarch
4 tbsp water
pepper to taste

1   Shred the pork and bamboo shoots into 2.5 cm (1 in) strips. Soak the dried mushrooms in hot water to cover for 25 minutes. Drain, reserving the soaking water. Discard the tough stalks from the mushrooms, then cut the caps into slices a similar size to the pork. Add the soaking water to the stock. Cut the tofu into 1.25 cm (½ in) cubes. Beat the egg lightly with a fork for 15 seconds. Roughly chop the scallions. Mix the hot and sour mixture together in a bowl.

2   Bring the stock to a boil in a wok or saucepan. Add the pork, carrot and mushrooms and simmer for 10 minutes. Add the fresh or frozen shrimp, tofu, bamboo shoots, salt, crumbled stock cubes, peas and scallions. Continue to cook for 3–4 minutes, then stir in the hot and sour mixture, which will thicken the soup. Gently pour the beaten egg over the surface of the soup in a thin stream. Sprinkle the soup with sesame oil and serve immediately.

Top-Rank Bird's Nest

Serves 4–6

60 g (2 oz) "bird's nest"

2 tsp Chinese alkali powder

1 litre (2 pt) chicken stock (see page 152)

1 tsp salt

½ tsp monosodium glutamate (optional)

1 tbsp rice wine or sherry

Cook's tip

The so-called "bird's nest" is in fact a pre-digested protein from a seaweed used by swallows for building their nests on the cliffs of island's along China's coast. They can often be found in Chinese herbal medicine shops and sometimes in Chinese grocery stores.

1 Soak the "nest" in lukewarm water for about 15 minutes and pick out all the feathers and other pieces with tweezers—this is where patience is required; then rinse very gently in lukewarm water two or three times.

2 Dissolve the alkali in 600 ml (1 pt) boiling water, then add the cleaned 'bird's nest' and stir gently with chopsticks or a fork. Leave it to stand for 5 minutes, then drain and soak in at least 1.25 litres (2¼ pt) fresh boiling water for 5 more minutes. Drain again. Finally rinse the "nest" in the same quantity of fresh warm water for 4 minutes more and drain well; by now it is clean and ready for the last stage of cooking.

3 Bring the chicken stock, salt, monosodium glutamate (if using) and rice wine or sherry to a boil, skim if necessary, then add the well drained "bird's nest" and serve immediately.

Yin and Yang Soup

Serves 4–6
550 g (1¼ lb) spinach leaves
1 tsp baking soda
230 g (8 oz) button mushrooms
110 g (4 oz) chicken breast, minced
1 egg white
2 tsp salt
4 tbsp groundnut oil
2 tsp Chinese yellow wine
1 litre (2 pt) chicken stock (see page 152)
3 tbsp cornstarch

1 Blanch the spinach for 2 minutes in 480 ml (1 pt) boiling water with 1 tsp baking soda added. Remove and rinse. Drain the leaves before chopping them finely. Chop the mushrooms and set aside. Mix the minced chicken breast with the egg white and 1 tsp salt.

2 Heat 2 tbsp oil in a pan. Sauté the spinach for 3 minutes, add 1 tsp Chinese yellow wine and 1 tsp salt and stir together. Mixed 3 tbsp of the stock with 3 tbsp cornstarch. Add 480 ml (1 pt) chicken stock to the saucepan. Bring the stock to a boil and slowly stir in the cornstarch-stock mixture.

3 Place an S-shaped piece of greased cardboard in the center of a large soup bowl to divide it in two. Pour the spinach soup into one side of the bowl, holding the cardboard upright by placing a glass of water against it on the empty side.

4 Heat 2 tbsp oil. Add the mushrooms, sauté for 1 minute and add 1 tsp Chinese yellow wine. Take 3 tbsp of the remaining stock and mix with the cornstarch. Add the rest of the chicken stock to the pan, bring to a boil and slowly stir in the blended cornstarch. When it boils, stir in the minced chicken and mix well.

5 Pour the chicken soup into the other half of the soup bowl, first removing the glass of water. Take out the cardboard as gently as possible. The one bowl of soup is then presented and served in the two colors of yin and yang.

Oxtail Soup

Serves 4–6
1 oxtail
230 g (8 oz) carrots
3.6 litres (7 pt) water
½ tbsp fresh ginger, crushed
1 tbsp Sichuan peppercorns
4 tbsp rice wine or sherry
1 chicken
salt to taste

1 Trim off the excess fat on the oxtail and cut into pieces. Cut the carrots into thick chunks.

2 Place the oxtail in a large pot with water, bring to a boil, skim off the scum; add root ginger, Sichuan peppercorns, wine or sherry and chicken. Reduce heat when it starts to boil, simmer for 4 hours or more, turning the chicken and oxtail over every hour or so. Add the carrots in the last 20 minutes of cooking time. Discard chicken before serving; add salt to taste.

Wonton Soup

Serves 4–6
¼ tbsp dried shrimp
1 tbsp groundnut oil
4 slices fresh ginger
1 litre (2 pt) chicken stock (see page 152)
2 tsp sugar
2 tsp sesame oil
4–6 tsp light soy sauce
2 tbsp scallions, chopped
40 wontons

1 Soak the dried shrimp in 300 ml (10 fl oz) hot water for 30 minutes. Heat 1 tbsp oil in a pot or casserole dish and add the ginger and dried shrimp, stirring until it starts to smell . Add the chicken stock plus the water used to soak the shrimp. Bring the contents to a boil, reduce the heat and simmer for 30 minutes. Add the sugar and keep warm in the pot.

2 Use four or six soup bowls and put into each ¼ tsp sesame oil, 1 tsp light soy sauce and 1 tsp chopped scallion. Set aside.

3 Bring 2.5 litre (5 pt) water to a boil. Add the wontons. Reduce the heat to medium and simmer for 5 minutes. Remove with a slotted spoon and divide them equally among the soup bowls. Add the soup and serve.

Spinach and Tofu Soup

Serves 4–6

230 g (8 oz) fresh spinach
2 cakes tofu
2 tbsp oil
2 tsp salt
600 ml (1 pt) water
2 tbsp soy sauce
1 tsp sesame oil

1. Wash the spinach well, discarding the tough and discolored leaves. Shake off the excess water and cut the leaves into small pieces.
2. Cut the tofu into about quarters. In a wok or large pot, heat the oil until hot. Stirfry the spinach until soft. Add the salt and water and bring to a boil.
3. Add the tofu and soy sauce and cook for 1½–2 minutes. Add the sesame oil just before serving.

Liver Pâté Soup

Serves 4–6

230 g (8 oz) pig's liver
700 ml (1½ pt) stock
2 egg whites
1 tbsp rice wine or sherry
1 tsp salt
salt and pepper to taste

1. Chop the liver into a pulp; squeeze it through muslin; mix it with 60 ml (2 fl oz) stock and the egg whites; add wine or sherry and salt. Place in a bowl, and steam for 15 minutes; by then it will have become a solid liver pâté; let it cool.
2. Place the liver pâté on the bottom of a large soup bowl; cut it into small squares (but keep the whole pieces together). Bring the stock to a boil and gently pour it over the liver. Season with salt and pepper, and serve.

Tomato and Egg Flower Soup

Serves 4–6

260 g (9 oz) tomatoes
1 egg
2 scallions, finely chopped
1 tbsp oil
1 litre (2 pt) water
2 tbsp light soy sauce
1 tsp cornstarch mixed with 2 tsp water

1. Skin the tomatoes by dipping them in boiling water for a minute or so and then peel them. Cut into large slices.
2. Beat the egg. Finely chop the scallions.
3. Heat a wok or frying pan over high heat. Add the oil and wait for it to smoke. Add the scallions to flavour the oil and then pour in the water. Drop in the tomatoes and bring to a boil. Add the soy sauce and very slowly pour in the beaten egg. Add the cornstarch and water mixture. Stir and serve.

Pork Dumplings

Serves 6–8
100 g (4 oz) all-purpose flour
2 eggs
¼ tsp baking soda

Filling
3 medium dried black mushrooms
560 g (1¼ lb) pork fillet
110 g (8 oz) pork fat

Marinade
1 tbsp light soy sauce
½ tsp sugar
½ tsp sesame oil
½ tsp pepper
1 tsp Chinese yellow wine
1 tbsp cornstarch
1 egg white
1 tsp salt

1 Make the wrappers for the dumplings by putting the flour in a mixing bowl. Make a well in the center, add the eggs and baking soda and mix well. Knead the dough on a lightly floured surface until it is smooth.

2 Roll the dough into a sausage shape approximately 3.5 cm (1½ in) in diameter, cover it with a tea towel and leave to stand for 20 minutes.

3 Pull the dough apart and roll the pieces between your palms into small balls approximately 2.5 cm (1 in) in diameter. Flatten each ball slightly, dust with flour and roll out into a thin pancake.

4 Soak the black mushrooms in hot water for 30 minutes. Cut off and discard the stems and finely dice the caps.

5 Cut the pork and pork fat into small cubes and mix with the mushroom pieces and the marinade ingredients, stirring with a fork until the mixture becomes sticky.

6 Place one wrapper in the palm of your hand. Put a heaped teaspoon of the filling in the center of the wrapper and squeeze the edges gently together until it looks like a purse, but leave the top open. If you wish, trim away any excess wrapper, but this is not essential. Continue until all the wrappers are used. Steam over high heat for 10–15 minutes. Serve.

Lotus Leaf Pancakes

Makes 24 pancakes
450 g (1 lb) all-purpose flour
300 ml (10 fl oz) boiling water
3 tsp vegetable oil

1 Sift the flour into a mixing bowl and very slowly pour in the boiling water, mixed with 1 tsp oil, while stirring with a pair of chopsticks or a wooden spoon. Do not be tempted to add any more water than the amount given, otherwise the mixture will get too wet and become messy.

2 Knead the mixture into a firm dough, then divide it into three equal portions. Now roll out each portion into a long sausage shape, and cut each sausage into eight equal parts; then, using the palm of your hand, press each piece into a flat pancake. Brush one of the pancakes with a little oil, and place another one on top to form a sandwich, so that you end up with 12 sandwiches. Now use a rolling pin to flatten each sandwich into a 15 cm (6 in) circle by rolling gently on each side on a lightly floured surface.

3 To cook, place a frying pan over high heat, and when it is hot reduce the heat to moderate. Put one pancake "sandwich" at a time into the ungreased saucepan, and turn it over when it starts to puff up with bubbles. It is done when little brown spots appear on the underside. Remove from the saucepan and very gently peel apart the 2 layers and fold each one in half.

4 If the pancakes are not to be served as soon as they are cooked, they can be stored and warmed up, either in a steamer or the oven for 5–10 minutes.

Won't Stick Three Ways

Serves 4–6
5 egg yolks
110 g (4 oz) sugar
2 tbsp cornstarch
5 tbsp water
3 tbsp lard

1 Beat the egg yolks and add sugar, cornstarch and water; blend well.

2 Heat the lard in a frying pan over high heat, tilt the pan so that the entire surface is covered in lard, then pour the excess lard (about half) into a container for later use. Reduce the heat to medium, pour the egg mixture into the pan, stir and scramble for about 2 minutes and add the remaining lard from the jug little by little, stirring and scrambling all the time until the eggs become bright golden, then serve.

Eight Treasure Dessert

Serves 6–8

560 g (1¼ lb) glutinous rice
1½ tbsp lard
75 g (3 oz) sugar
25–35 g (1½ oz) nuts (almonds, walnuts,
    chestnuts or lotus seeds)
6 tbsp candied or dried fruits (optional)
about 1½ tbsp sweet bean paste

1   Wash the rice and place in a saucepan. Cover
    with 1.25 cm (½ in) water. Bring to a boil and
    simmer gently for 11–12 minutes. Add half of the
    lard and all of the sugar, turn and stir until well
    mixed. Grease the sides of a large heatproof bowl
    heavily with the remaining lard (it must be cold).
    Stick the nuts and fruits of your choice in a pattern
    on the sides of the bowl in the lard, arranging
    the remainder at the bottom of the bowl. Place a
    layer of sweetened rice in the bowl, then spread
    a thinner layer of sweet bean paste on top of the
    rice. Repeat the layers, finishing with a rice layer.
    Cover the bowl with foil, leaving a little room for
    expansion.
2   Place the bowl into a steamer and steam
    steadily for 1 hour 10 minutes until cooked. Invert
    the bowl onto a large round heated serving dish to
    turn out the dessert. Decorate with extra candied
    fruits (optional).

Sa Chi Ma

Serves 4–6

125 g (5 oz) flour
2 tsp baking powder
3 eggs
oil for deep frying
225 g (8 oz) sugar
180 ml (6 fl oz) honey
240 ml (8 fl oz) water

1   Sift flour and baking powder onto a pastry board.
    Spread to form a hollow in the center; add eggs,
    blend well. Knead the dough thoroughly until it is
    smooth.
2   Roll the dough with a rolling pin until it is like a big
    pancake about 3 mm (⅛ in) in thickness. Cut it into
    5 cm (2 in) long thin strips; dust strips with flour so
    they won't stick.
3   Heat the oil and deep fry the thin strips in batches
    for 45 seconds until light golden. Remove. Drain.
4   Place the sugar, honey and water in a saucepan;
    bring it to a boil over high heat; simmer and stir
    until the mixture is like syrup. Add the thin strips
    and mix thoroughly until each strip is coated
    with syrup. Turn it out into a pre-greased tin and
    press to form one big piece. When cool, cut it into
    squares with a sharp knife.

Toffee Bananas

Serves 4

4 bananas, peeled
1 egg
2 tbsp all-purpose flour
oil for deep frying
4 tbsp sugar
1 tbsp cold water

1 Cut the bananas in half lengthways and then cut each half into two crossways.
2 Beat the egg, add the flour and mix well to make a smooth batter.
3 Heat the oil in a wok or deep fryer. Coat each piece of banana with batter and deep fry until golden. Remove and drain.
4 Pour off the excess oil, leaving about 1 tbsp of oil in the wok. Add the sugar and water and stir over medium heat to dissolve the sugar. Continue stirring and when the sugar has caramelized, add the hot banana pieces. Coat well and remove. Dip the hot bananas in cold water to harden the toffee and serve immediately.

Index

Index

Acknowledgements

The publishers would like to thank the following picture libraries for their kind permission to use their pictures:

Istock: 28, 31, 40, 167, 172

Shutterstock: front cover, 4, 5, 7, 13, 19, 20, 22, 23, 24, 30, 32, 34, 38, 42, 43, 44, 46, 47, 49, 52, 53, 54, 57, 58, 63, 64, 67, 68, 69, 71, 72, 76, 78, 81, 84, 87, 88, 89, 91, 93, 95, 98, 99, 101, 102, 103, 109, 110, 111, 114, 116, 120, 122, 125, 129, 133, 134, 138, 139, 140, 141, 151, 153

Photocuisine: 25, 56

Stockfood: 15, 27, 33, 75, 97, 160, 161

Every effort has been made to contact the copyright holders for images reproduced in this book. The Publisher would welcome any errors or omissions being brought to their attention and apologizes in advance for any unintentional omissions or errors. The Publisher will be pleased to insert the appropriate acknowledgement to any companies or individuals in any subsequent edition of the work.